PEARSON ALWAYS LEARNING

Bill Wright

Physics Lab Manual

Custom Second Edition

Cover Art: Courtesy of Photodisc/Getty Images.

Pearson Learning Solutions, 501 Boylston Street, Suite 900, Boston, MA 02116
A Pearson Education Company
www.pearsoned.com

Printed in the United States of America

6 7 8 9 10 V3NL 17 16 15 14 13

000200010271278015

RG

ISBN 10: 1-256-47751-6
ISBN 13: 978-1-256-47751-8

TABLE OF CONTENTS

		Page No.
LAB 1	GRAPHING AND ANALYSIS	1–10
LAB 2	KINEMATICS IN ONE DIMENSION	11–24
LAB 3	FORCES	25–44
LAB 4	ENERGY	45–58
LAB 5	TWO-DIMENSIONAL MOTION	59–68
LAB 6	GAS PROPERTIES	69–80
LAB 7	TEMPERATURE AND HEAT	81–90
LAB 8	ELECTRICITY	91–102
LAB 9	WAVES	103–114
LAB 10	QUANTUM THEORY	115–122
LAB 11	ELECTROMAGNETIC LAB	123–132
TROUBLESHOOTING		133–142

ABOUT THE AUTHOR

Bill Wright earned his B.S. in Physics from the University of Cincinnati. He earned his M.S. in Molecular Physics in 1995 from Wright State University for his work on electron mobility studies in CHF_3. He has been an instructor in post secondary education for fifteen years. He has teaching positions at Northern Kentucky University, ITT Technical Institute, and Sinclair University. He has developed and implemented virtual physics labs for the past five years at the University of Northern Kentucky and ITT Technical Institute.

ACKNOWLEDGEMENTS

Special thanks to Dr. Gregory Sobko for his writing contributions, and to both Dr. Gregory Sobko and Jimmy Alcock for their technical review of this lab manual.

1

GRAPHING AND ANALYSIS

PURPOSE

The purpose of this lab is to investigate the relationship between displacement and force in springs and to practice acquiring data then representing the tabulated data as a graph. You will use measurement data to identify unknown masses.

SIMULATION: MASSES AND SPRINGS

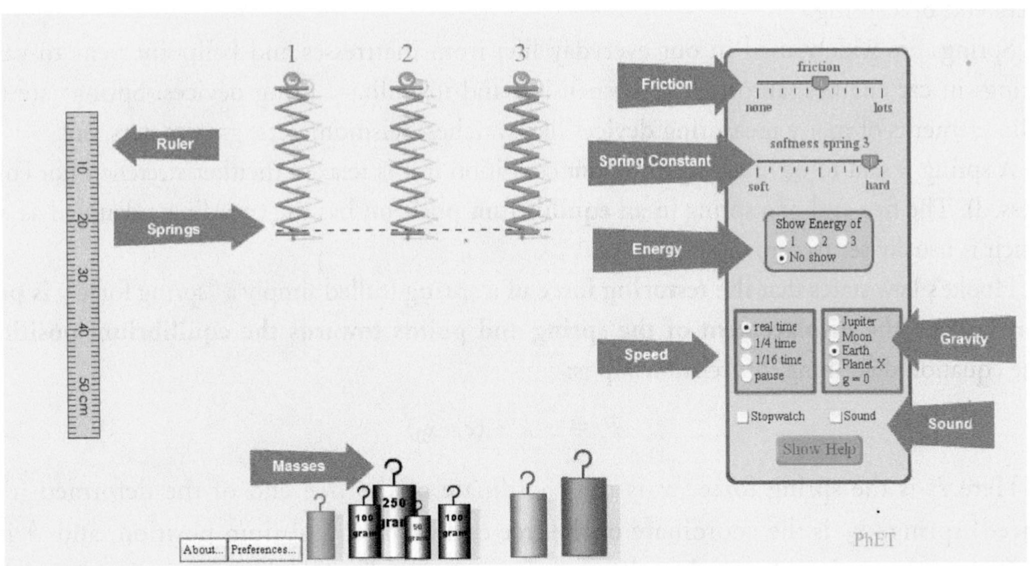

Figure 1-1

Feature	Control
Ruler	Move the ruler around by left-clicking then dragging and dropping it.
Springs	You can place masses on any of the three springs labeled 1, 2, and 3.
Spring Constant	The *softness spring 3* bar controls the stiffness of the 3rd spring. Move it right to increase the stiffness. Move it left to reduce the stiffness of the spring.
Energy	This feature will not be used in the lab. Leave the setting on *No show*.
Masses	You can move each mass by left-clicking then dragging and dropping it. Align the hooks with the end of the spring.
Friction	Moving the *friction* slider bar to the right increases friction. Moving the *friction* slider bar to the left reduces the friction.
Gravity	The gravity feature allows you to select the gravity used in the experiment.
Speed	Slow down the animation by selecting 1/4 time or 1/16 time.
Sound	Check the box to turn the sound on; uncheck the box to turn the sound off.

INTRODUCTION

A **spring** is an elastic object used to store mechanical energy. A spring-mass system includes a cylindrical, helical (coiled) spring fixed on one end and a body (mass) attached to the other (free) end of a spring.

Springs are widely used in our everyday life: from mattresses and ballpoint pens to valve springs in car engines, automobiles suspension and in military firing devices. Springs are the main elements of many measuring devices like watches, seismometers, gravimeters, etc.

A spring is said to be in **an equilibrium** condition if it is relaxed (neither stretched nor compressed). The free end of a spring in an **equilibrium position** has the coordinate denoted as x_0, which is usually set to zero: $x_0 = 0$.

Hooke's Law states that **the restoring force of a spring** (called simply a "spring force") **is proportional to the displacement of the spring and points towards the equilibrium position.** The equation describing this relationship is:

$$F_s = -k \cdot (x - x_0)$$

Here F_s is the spring force, x is the coordinate of the free end of the deformed (displaced) spring, x_0 is the coordinate of the free end in an equilibrium position, and k is a **spring constant** that shows the stiffness of the spring (how rigid or soft the spring is). Notice that if $x_0 = 0$, then Hooke's Law takes the simplified form: $F_s = -k \cdot x$. An applied force (a deforming force) is pointed in the opposite direction, as shown by the opposite sign of k:

$$F_a = k \cdot (x - x_0)$$

Hooke's Law establishes a direct proportionality between the magnitude of the applied force and the displacement of the spring from its equilibrium position. Graphically, this law will be represented in the Force-Displacement coordinate system by a straight line in which the slope is a spring constant.

In this lab, the force of gravity on a mass attached to the spring is an applied (deforming) force. You will use the collected data after running the simulation to graph the relationship between the applied force and the displacement of the mass attached to the spring (or, equivalently, between the developed spring force and the corresponding displacement).

PROCEDURES

Part 1

1. Apply the settings for the simulation as shown in Figure 1-2.
2. Without a mass attached to either Spring 1 or Spring 3, use the ruler to determine equilibrium—the starting position—for Spring 1 and Spring 3. To determine the starting position, place the ruler next to one of the springs. The starting position is the number on the ruler that aligns with the dashed line.

   Let x_{0S1} represent the starting position of Spring 1 and x_{0S3} represent the starting position of Spring 3. For the example shown in Figure 1-3, $x_{0S1} = 10\text{cm}$ and $x_{0S3} = 20\text{cm}$

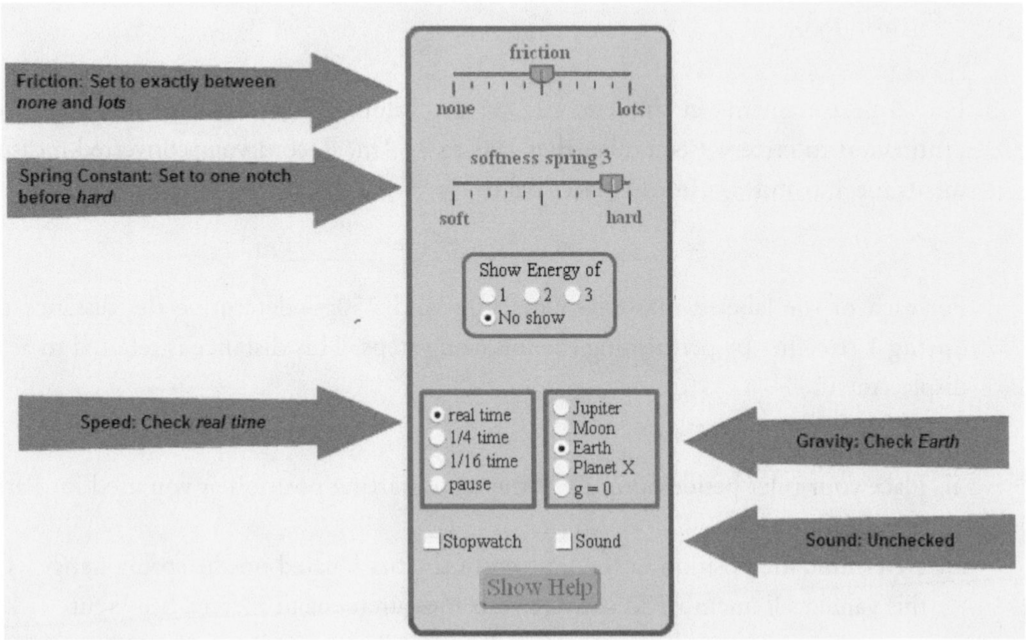

Figure 1-2

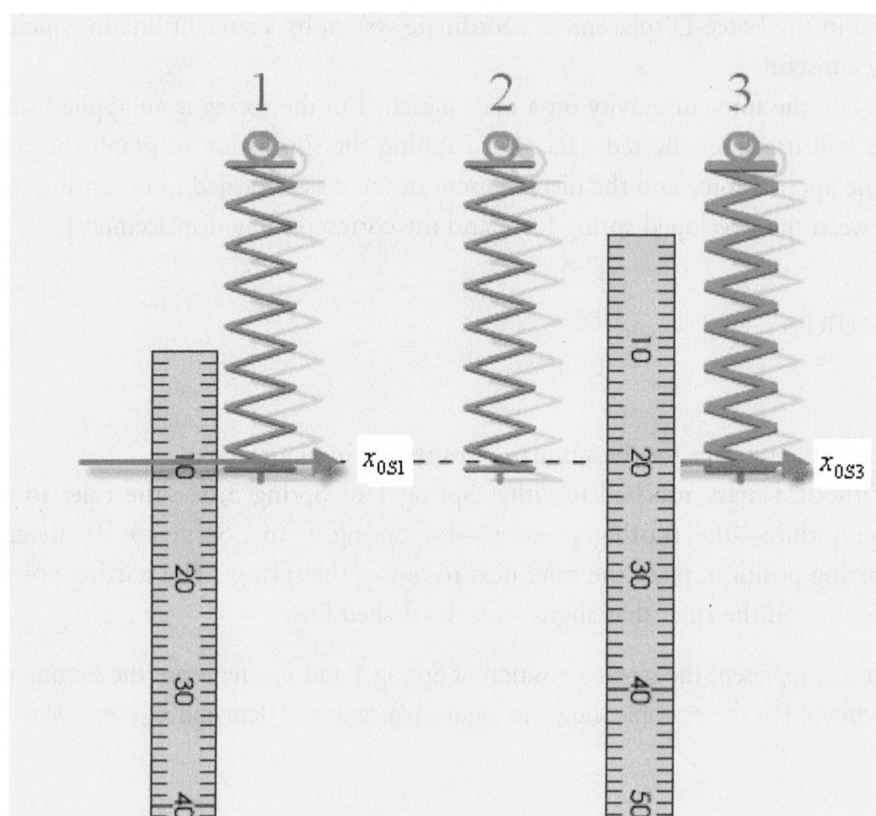

Figure 1-3

3. For all measurements in this lab, convert the values you measure on the ruler from centimeters to meters. Remember that 100cm = 1m. Record your converted measurements for x_{0S1} and x_{0S3} in the spaces below.

$$x_{0S1} = \_\_\_\_\_\_ \text{ m} \qquad x_{0S3} = \_\_\_\_\_\_ \text{ m}$$

4. For each of the labeled masses—50g, 100g, and 250g—determine the distance that **Spring 1** stretches by performing the following steps. This distance is referred to as the displacement.

   i. Attach the mass.
   ii. Place your ruler beside Spring 1 at the same starting position as you used for Part 1, Step 3 of this lab.
   iii. Determine the position of the bottom of the bar located on the spring hanger. Call this value x. Remember to convert your measurement to meters. See Figure 1-4.

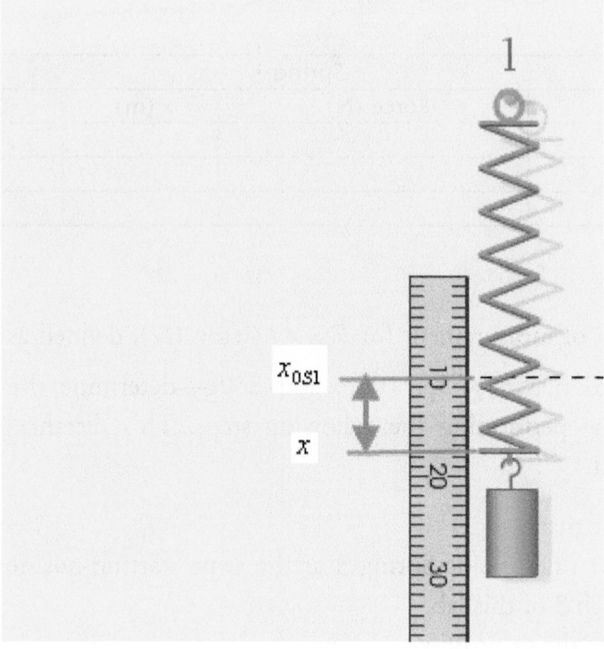

Figure 1-4

iv. Record your answers in Table 1-1.

v. Subtract x_{0S1} from x to determine the displacement. Record your value for displacement in Table 1-1.

In the example shown in Figure 1-4, displacement is calculated as follows:

$$\begin{aligned}\text{Displacement} &= 17.5\text{cm} - 10\text{cm}\\ &= 7.5\text{cm}\\ &= 0.075\text{m}\end{aligned}$$

5. Calculate the applied force F (gravity) by using the formula: $F = ma$. In this case, a (the acceleration) is due to gravity. Gravitational acceleration is $9.8\frac{m}{s^2}$, which you will substitute that into the formula for force. Here the unit of measurement for F is a newton (N), defined as $N = \frac{kg \cdot m}{s^2}$. Because this formula requires the use of kilograms, convert the mass from grams to kilograms. (Remember 1000g = 1kg.) Record your answers in Table 1-1.

Table 1-1

Spring 1			
Mass (g)	Force (N)	*x* (m)	Displacement (m)
50			
100			
250			

6. Here the unit of measurement for F is a newton (N), defined as $N = \frac{kg \cdot m}{s^2}$. For each of the labeled masses—50g, 100g, and 250g—determine the distance that Spring 3 stretches by performing the following steps. This distance is referred to as **the displacement.**

   i. Attach the mass.
   ii. Place your ruler beside Spring 3 at the same starting position as you used for the Part 1, Step 3 of this lab.
   iii. Determine the value of x.
   iv. Record your answers in Table 1-1.
   v. Subtract x_{0S3} from x. Record your value for displacement in Table 1-2.

7. Calculate the force applied by gravity (on earth) by multiplying the mass (in kilograms) by 9.8. Record your answers in Table 1-2.

Table 1-2

Spring 3			
Mass (g)	Force (N)	*x* (m)	Displacement (m)
50			
100			
250			

8. Use the blank graph paper in Figure 1-5 to plot the displacement and Force for both Spring 1 and Spring 3. Use different colored ink to draw each graph and label the lines appropriately.

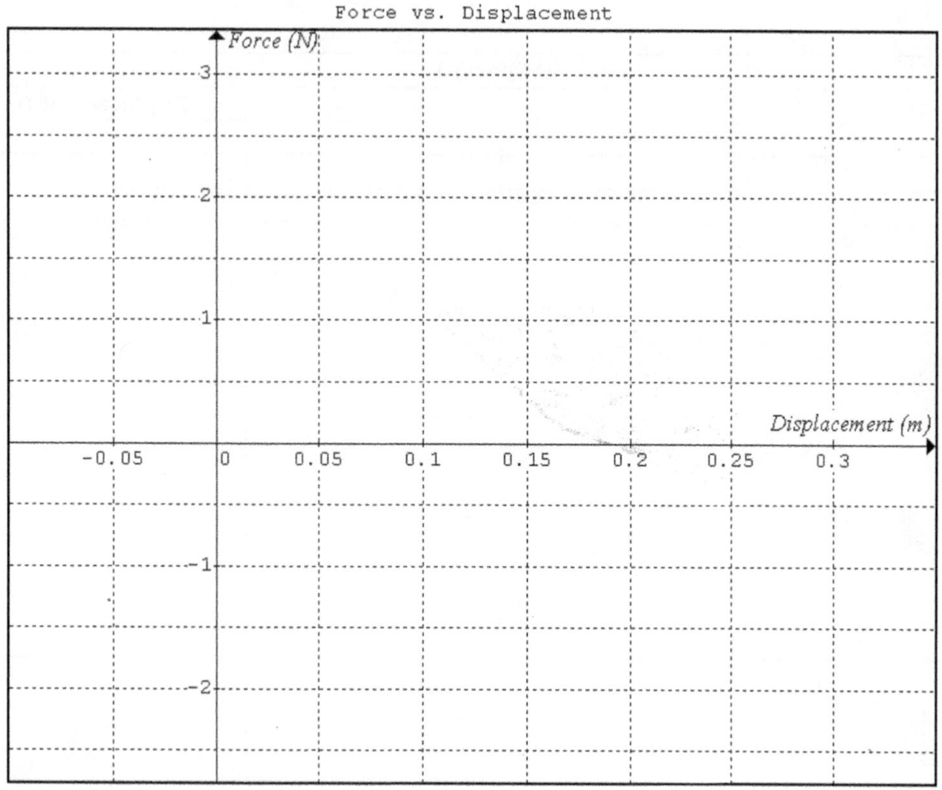

Figure 1-5

Part 2

1. Use the information you collected in Part 1, Step 5 of this lab to complete the first three rows of Table 1-3.
2. Attach each of the masses without labels to Spring 1. Record the displacement stretched in Table 1-3.
3. Use the Force vs. Position graph you plotted for Spring 1 in Part 1, Step 8 of this lab to find the forces for the unknown masses. Record you results in Table 1-3.
4. Identify the unknown masses, Unknown 1, Unknown 2, and Unknown 3, by performing the following steps:

   i. Use the forces you recorded in Part 2, Step 3 of this lab and divide the value by 9.8 to calculate the mass in kilograms.

   ii. Multiply the results by 1000 to convert the values to grams. Record your results in Table 1-3.

Table 1-3

Spring 1		
Mass (g)	**Force (N)**	**Displacement (m)**
50		
100		
250		
Unknown 1 = _______		
Unknown 2 = _______		
Unknown 3 = _______		

QUESTIONS

1. What kind of dependence—direct proportionality, inverse, inverse square, or power relationship—do you observe between the applied force and displacement?

2. The slope of the lines on the graphs represents the spring's stiffness. What does this information this tell you about the two springs?

3. Create a linear equation that represents the relationship between Force (N) and displacement (m) for both Spring 1 and Spring 3. Use the graph you created in Figure 1-4.
(Hint: Use the slope and y-intercept.)

2

KINEMATICS IN ONE DIMENSION

PURPOSE

The purpose of this lab is to investigate the relationships between the kinematic quantities of velocity, position, and acceleration.

SIMULATIONS

Forces in One Dimension

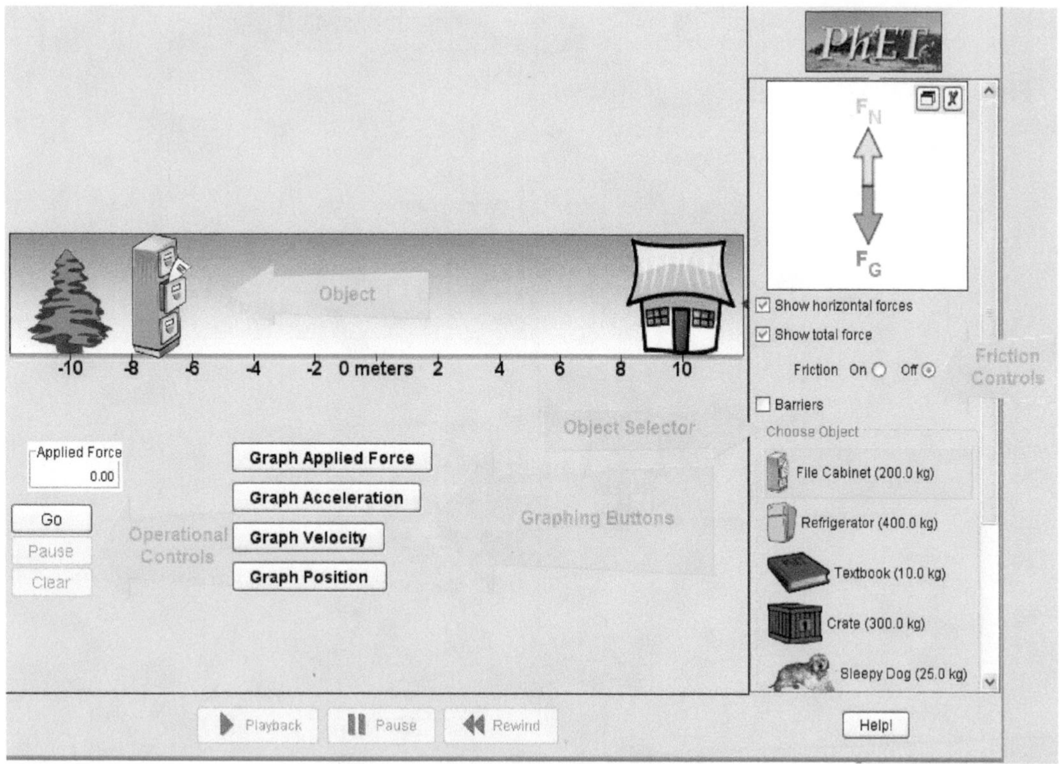

Figure 2-1

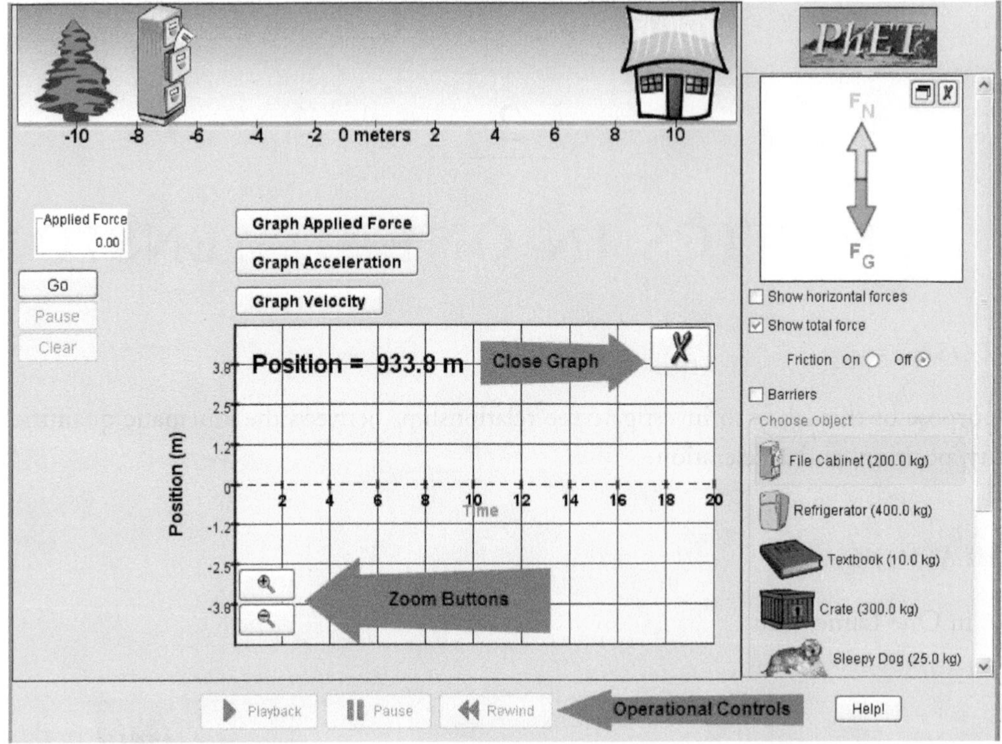

Figure 2-2

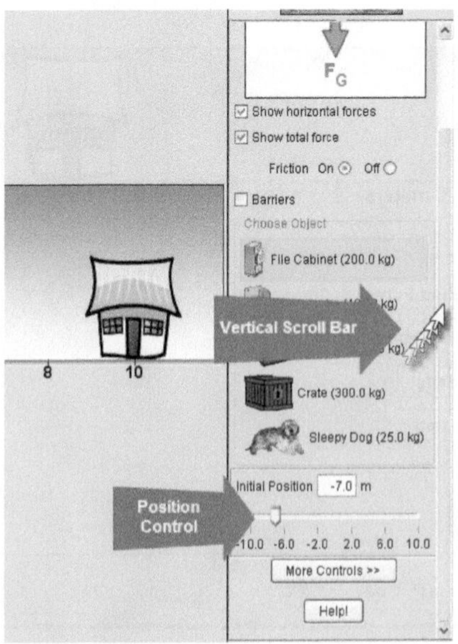

Figure 2-3

Feature	Control
	Figure 2-1
Object	• To move an object to the right, depress and hold down the left mouse button while dragging the cursor to the right of the object. Drag the cursor over a few units and do not release the button until the specified time has elapsed. • To move an object to the left, depress and hold down the left mouse button while dragging the cursor to the left of the object. Drag the cursor over a few units and do not release the button until the specified time has elapsed.
Graphing Buttons	These buttons turn the graphs on and off.
Spring Constant	Turn this option on or off to control friction.
Friction Control	This allows you to select the object you will use.
Operational Controls	Pause suspends the animation. Go un-pauses the animation. Clear resets the graphs.
	Figure 2-2
Zoom Buttons	Once you select a graph button, a graph will appear on the screen. You may change the scaling by clicking on a magnifying glass; (–) allows you to increase the range (zoom out) and (+) allows you to decrease the range (zoom in).
	Click this button to close a graph.
Operational Controls	Click Rewind to replay your graph from the beginning. Click Playback after Rewind to start the replay. Click Pause to stop the reply at any time. This pause will button will also stop the animation if it is the first time to run it.
	Figure 2-3
Position Control	Click and drag the *Vertical Scroll Bar* downward until you see the *Position Control.* Position the bar to move your object to its desired initial position.
More Controls	Locate the More Controls button by moving the Vertical Scroll Bar downward. See Figure 2-4. Click the More Controls button and you can find detail on data such as gravity and mass. See Figure 2-5. 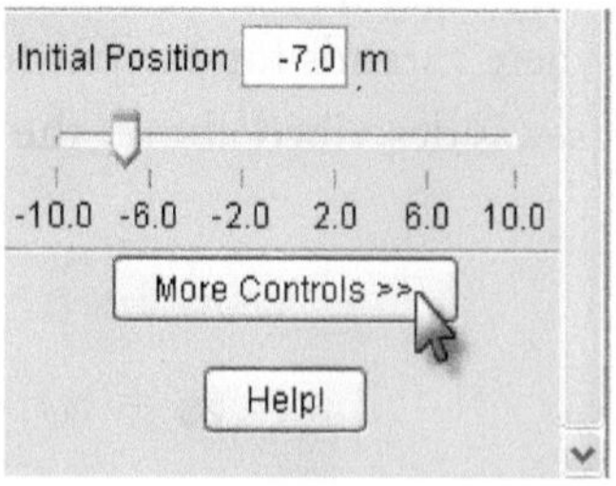 **Figure 2-4**

Continues

Feature	Control
More Controls	Gravity 9.8 N/kg Moon Earth Jupiter Mass 200.0 kg 0.1 500.0 1000.0 Figure 2-5

INTRODUCTION

Kinematics is a part of mechanics dealing with mathematical description of motion. It does not concern the causes of the motion or changes in the motion. Kinematic equations describe motion using variable quantities like position, velocity, acceleration, and time.

The following basic kinematic equations are used to model one-dimensional motion:

$$x = x_0 + v_{av}(t - t_0)$$

$$v = v_0 + a_{av}(t - t_0)$$

$$v^2 = v_0^2 + 2a_{av}(x - x_0)$$

$$x = x_0 + v_0(t - t_0) + \frac{1}{2}a_{av}(t - t_0)^2$$

where t_0, x_0, and v_0 denote initial time, initial position, and initial velocity, respectively, and v_{av} and a_{av} denote average values of velocity and acceleration, respectively.

If velocity v remains constant, then $v_{av} = v$, and if acceleration is constant, then $a_{av} = a$.

The formula $\Delta t = t - t_0$ represents the time elapsed after the initial time, t_0. If $t_0 = 0$, then $\Delta t = t$, where t stands for current (or final) time.

With the conditions set as described above, the equations you will use in this lab are:

$$v = v_0 + at$$

$$x - x_0 = v_0 t + \frac{1}{2}at^2$$

$$v^2 = v_0^2 + 2ax$$

In this lab, you will use data from the experiment to solve equations that can be used to predict the motion of the object. You will investigate the relationships between position, velocity, and acceleration.

PROCEDURES

Part 1

1. Apply the following settings for the simulation:

   a. Maximize the screen.
   b. Turn **on** the velocity, position, and acceleration graphs.
   c. Turn **off** the friction.
   d. Select the file cabinet for the object.
   e. Slide the position control to **−8m**.

   If you have correctly applied the settings, your screen will look similar to Figure 2-6.

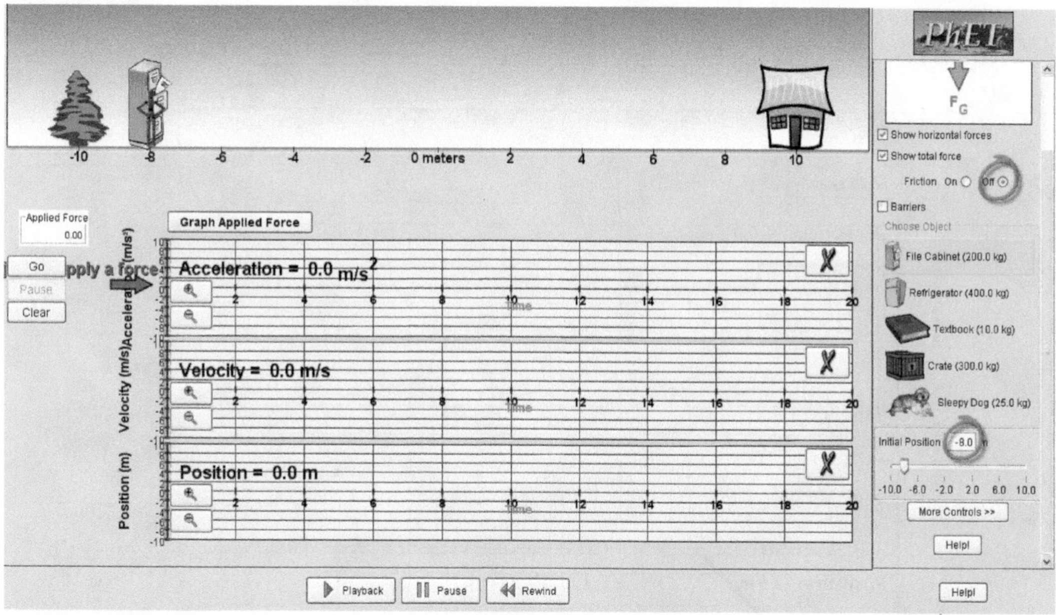

Figure 2-6

2. Apply a force by depressing and holding down the left mouse button while dragging the cursor to the right of the object—as shown in Figure 2-7. Release the button after four seconds. After four more seconds, click the pause button. Your screen will look similar (but not identical) to Figure 2-7.
3. Draw graphs for position, velocity, and acceleration using the data collected from the respective graphs generated by the simulation. Use the graph paper located at the end of this lab.

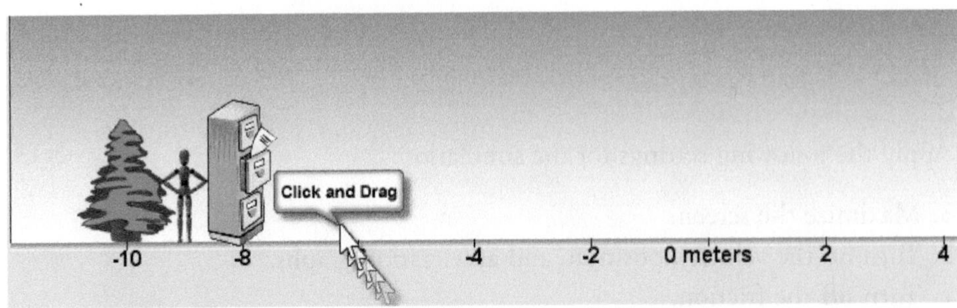

Figure 2-7

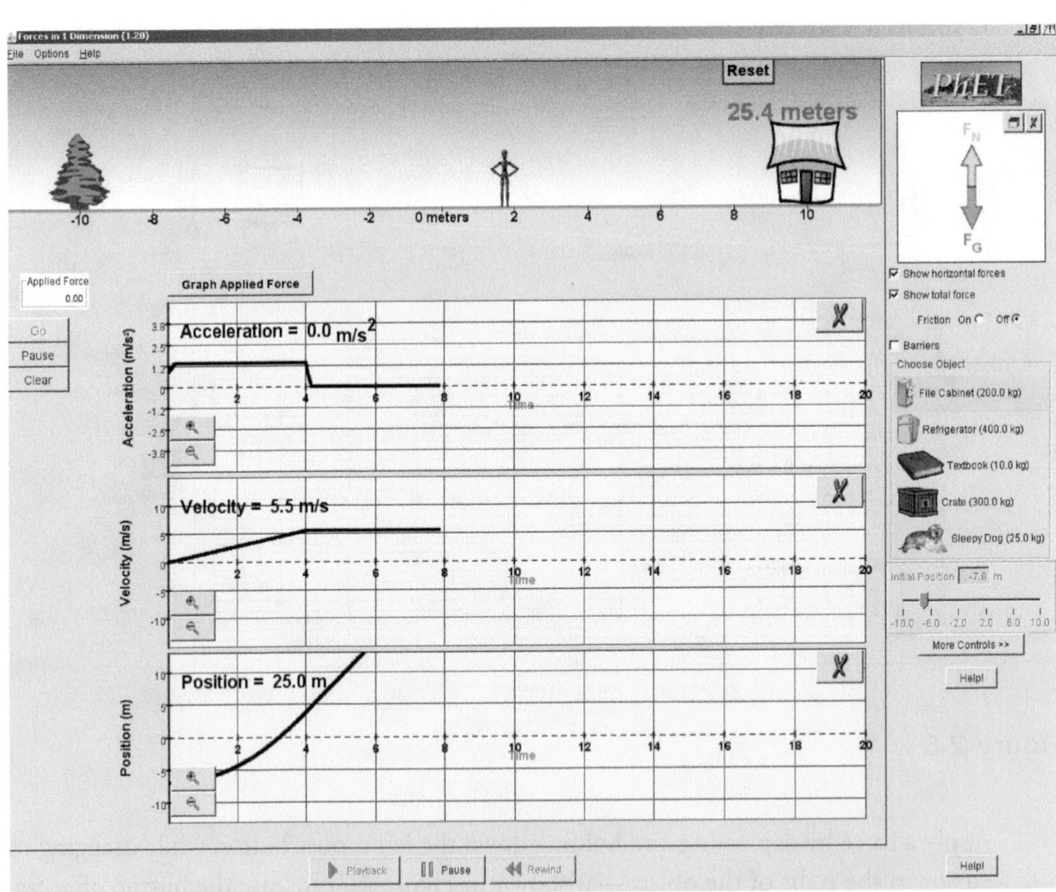

Figure 2-8

4. Use the graphs you completed in the previous step to answer the following questions using the time interval from 2 to 3 seconds:

   a. What type of curves—linear or parabolic—do you see in each of the graphs?

      i. Position vs. Time: ____________________
      ii. Velocity vs. Time: ____________________
      iii. Acceleration vs. Time: ____________________

   b. What is your position at $t = 2s$ (the initial position)?

   $x_0 =$ ________ m

5. What is your position at $t = 3s$ (the final position)?

   a. $x =$ ________ m

   b. What is your velocity at $t = 2s$ (the initial velocity)?

   $v_0 =$ ________ $\frac{m}{s}$

   c. Calculate the acceleration of the object for an elapsed time of $t = 1s$. Use the formula $x - x_0 = v_0t + \frac{1}{2}at^2$ and the values for x_0, x, and v_0 that you identified in the previous step.

   $a =$ ________ $\frac{m}{s^2}$

   d. Use your graph of Acceleration vs. Time to find the acceleration at $t = 3s$.

   $a =$ ________ $\frac{m}{s^2}$

   e. Calculate the velocity of the object for an elapsed time of $t = 1s$. Use the formula $v = v_0 + at$, the value for v_0, and the value for acceleration you determined in previous steps.

   $v =$ ________ $\frac{m}{s}$

   f. Use your graph of Velocity vs. Time to find the velocity at $t = 3s$.

   $v =$ ________ $\frac{m}{s}$

6. Click the clear button and start the simulation over. Apply the force to the right, holding the motion for 3 seconds, then immediately apply the force to the left for 3 more seconds. Release the button. Your screen should look similar to that shown in Figure 2-9.

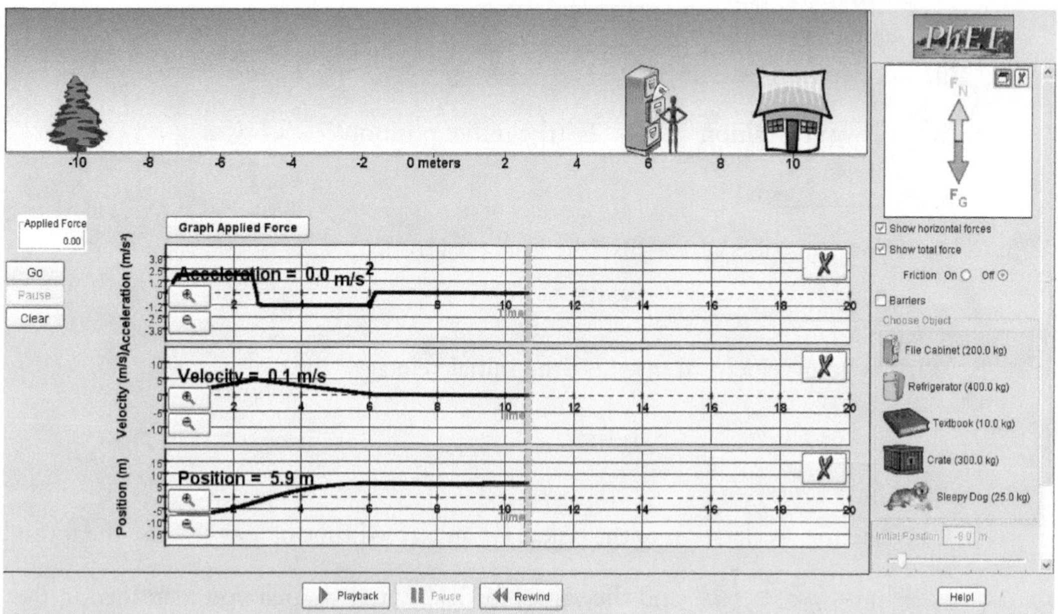

Figure 2-9

7. Draw graphs for position, velocity, and acceleration using the data collected from the respective graphs generated by the simulation. Use the graph paper located at the end of this lab.
8. Use the graphs you completed in the previous step to answer the following questions using the time interval from 4 to 5 seconds:

   a. What type of curves—linear or parabolic—do you see in each of the graphs?

      i. Position vs. Time: ____________________
      ii. Velocity vs. Time: ____________________
      iii. Acceleration vs. Time: ____________________

   b. What is your position at t = 4s (the initial position)?

      x_0 = ________ m

c. What is your final position at $t = 5$s (the final position)?

$x =$ _______ m

d. What is your velocity at $t = 4$s (the initial velocity)?

$v_0 =$ _______ $\frac{m}{s}$

e. Calculate the acceleration of the object for an elapsed time of $t = 1s$. Use the formula $x - x_0 = v_0 t + \frac{1}{2}at^2$ and the values for x_0, x, and v_0 that you identified in the previous step.

$a =$ _______ $\frac{m}{s^2}$

f. Use your graph of Acceleration vs. Time to find the acceleration at $t = 5s$.

$a =$ _______ $\frac{m}{s^2}$

g. Calculate the velocity of the object for an elapsed time of $t = 1s$ (final velocity). Use the formula, $v = v_0 + at$ the value for v_0, and the value for acceleration you determined in previous steps.

Final velocity $=$ _______ $\frac{m}{s}$

h. Use your graph of Velocity vs. Time to find the final velocity at $t = 5s$.

Final velocity $=$ _______ $\frac{m}{s}$

Part 2

1. Repeat Part I, Step 2 with a different object selected.
2. Draw graphs for position, velocity, and acceleration using the data collected from the respective graphs generated by the simulation. Use the graph paper located at the end of this lab.

QUESTIONS

1. Did you see any differences in the graphs between the two different objects?

2. How did your calculated values for acceleration and velocity compare to the graphed values?

3. Is it possible to have negative values for any of the kinematic variables of position, velocity, and acceleration (at any time)? If so, describe what type of motion can result in negative values.

Part 1 Step 3 Graphs

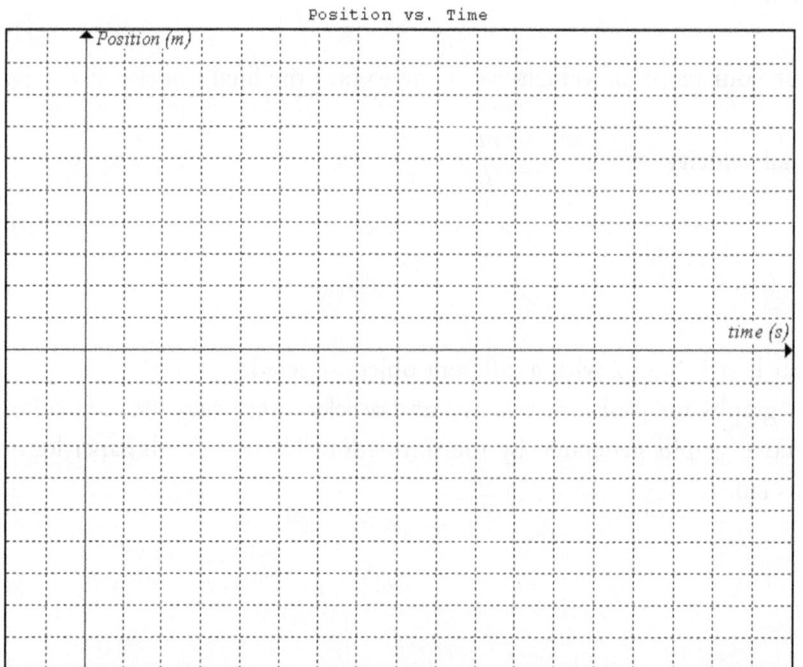

Velocity vs. Time

Velocity (m/s)

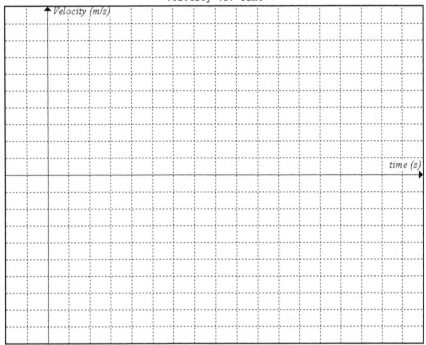

time (s)

Acceleration vs. Time

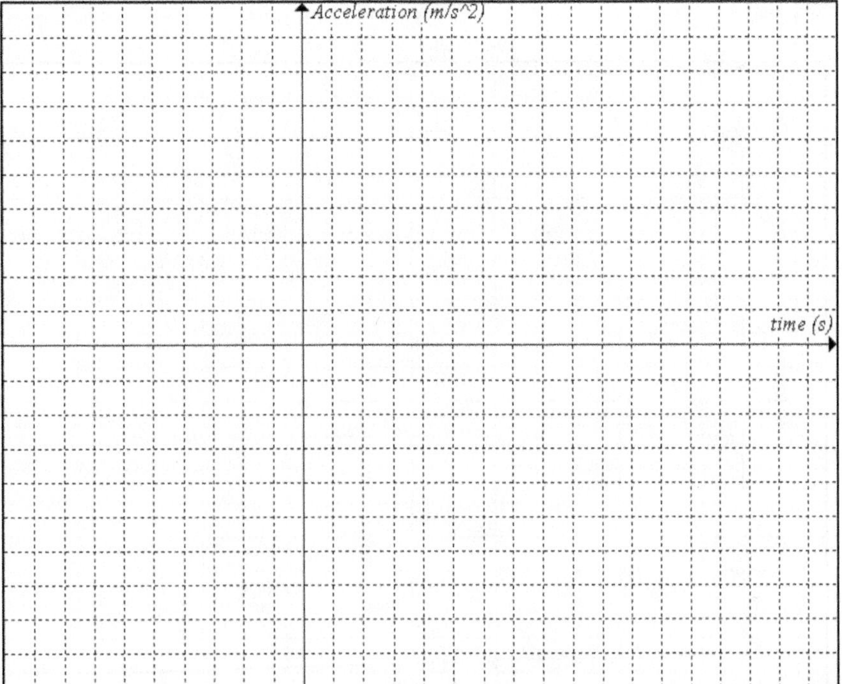

Part 1 Step 7 Graphs

Position vs. Time

Position (m)

time (s)

Velocity vs. Time

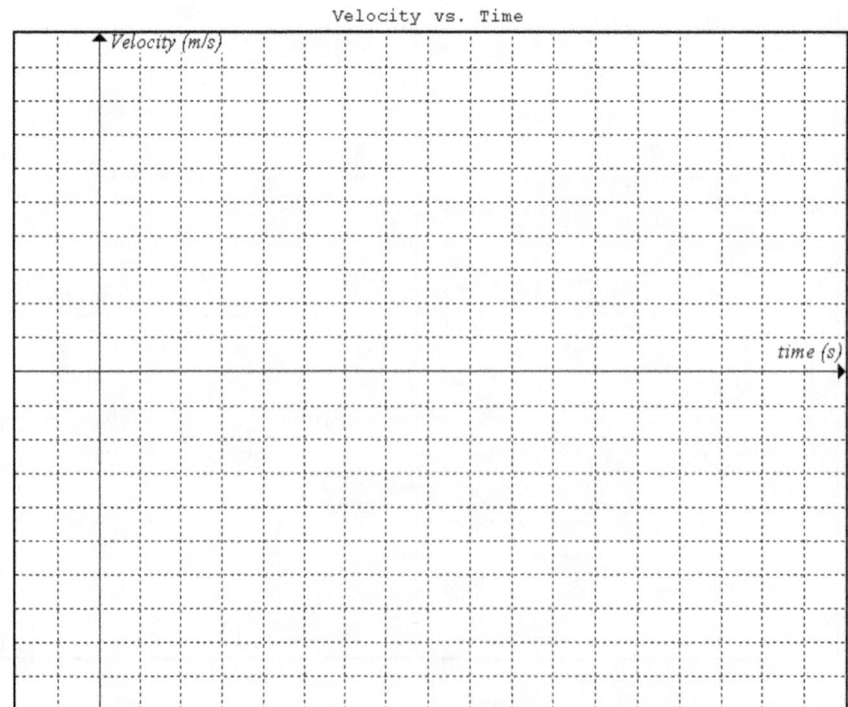

Acceleration vs. Time

Acceleration (m/s^2)

time (s)

Part 2 Step 2 Graphs

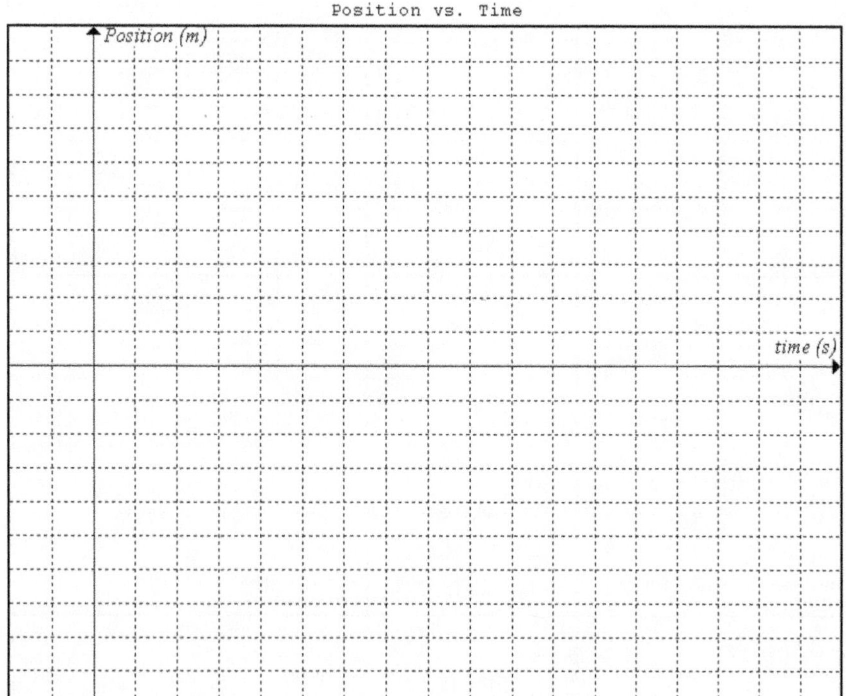

Velocity vs. Time

Velocity (m/s)

time (s)

Acceleration vs. Time

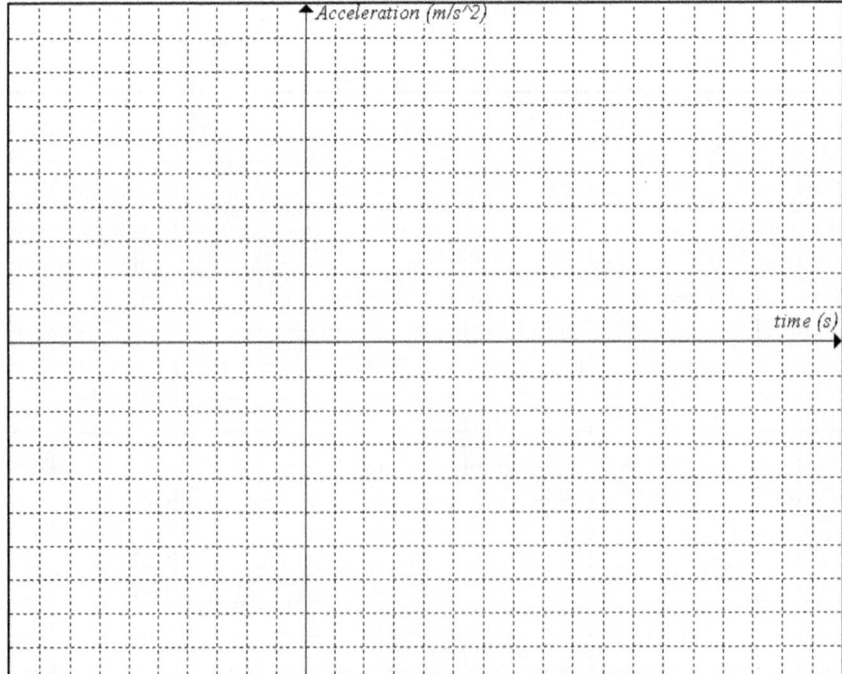

3

FORCES

PURPOSE

The purpose of this lab is to investigate the relationship between force and the kinematic quantity of acceleration.

SIMULATIONS

Forces in One Dimension

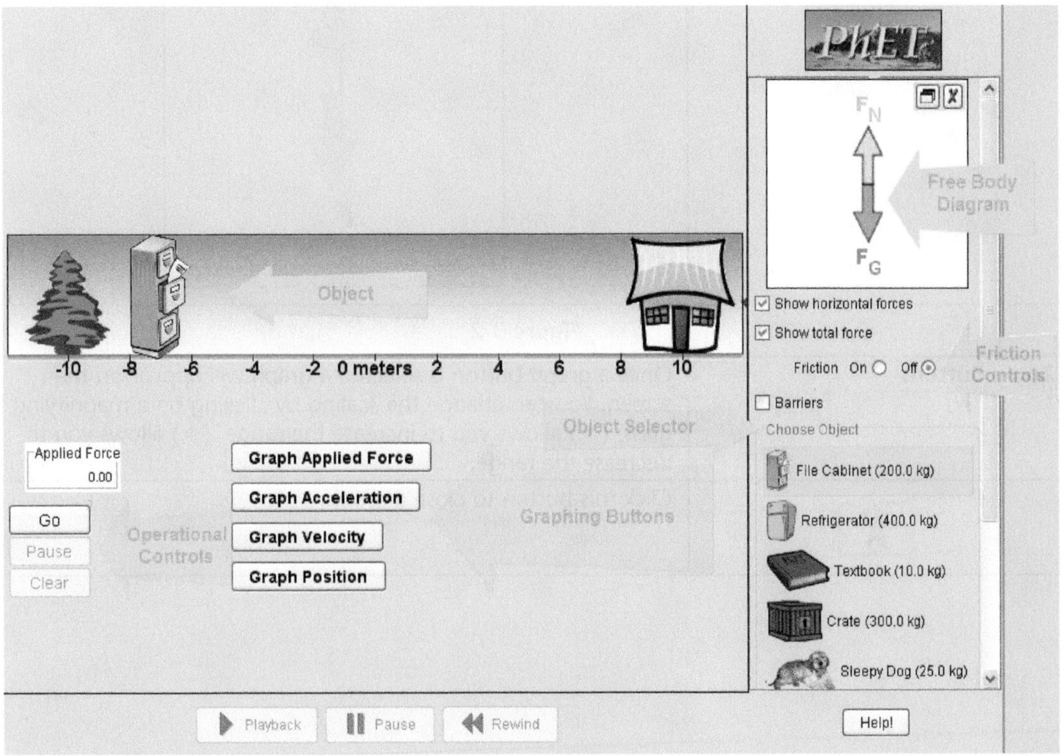

Figure 3-1

Feature	Control
Figure 3-1	
Object	• To move an object to the right, depress and hold down the left mouse button while dragging the cursor to the right of the object. Drag the cursor over a few units and do not release the button until the specified time has elapsed. • To move an to the left, depress and hold down the left mouse button while dragging the cursor to the left of the object. Drag the cursor over a few units and do not release the button until the specified time has elapsed.
Graphing Buttons	These buttons turn the graphs on and off.
Spring Constant	This option can be selected on or off to control friction.
Friction Control	This allows you to select the object you will use.
Operational Controls	Pause will suspend the animation and Go un-pauses the animation. Clear will reset the graphs.
Free Body Diagram	Enable the Free Body Diagram for this simulation. When it is enabled, the following graphic should appear.
Figure 3-2	
Zoom Buttons	Once a graph button is selected a graph will appear on the screen. You can change the scaling by clicking on a magnifying glass; (−) allows you to increase the range, (+) allows you to decrease the range.
	Click this button to close a graph.

Feature	Control
Operational Controls	Click Rewind to replay your graph from the beginning. Click Playback after Rewind to start the replay. Click Pause if you want to stop the replay at a particular point in time. 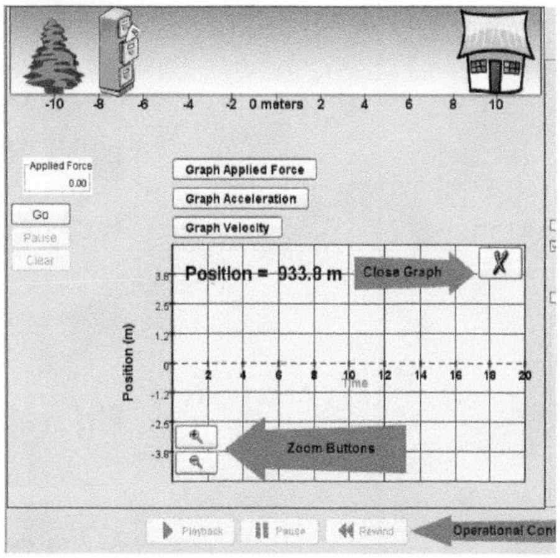 Figure 3-2
Figure 3-3	
Position Control	Click and drag the scroll bar down until you see the position control. Position the bar to move your object to its desired initial position. 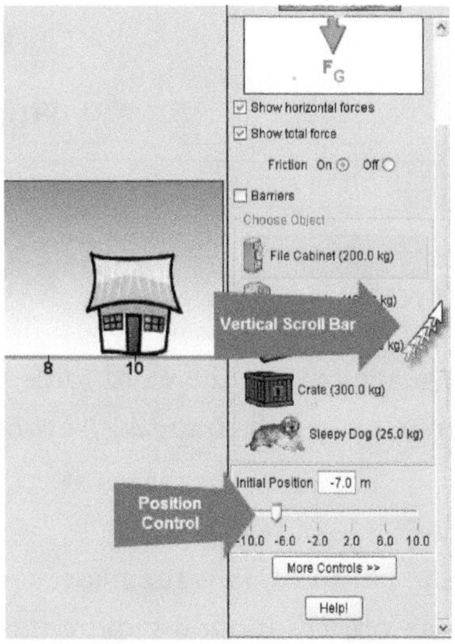 Figure 3-3

Continues

Feature	Control
More Controls	Locate the More Controls button by moving the Vertical Scroll Bar downward. See Figure 2-4. Click the More Controls button and you can find detail on data such as gravity and mass. 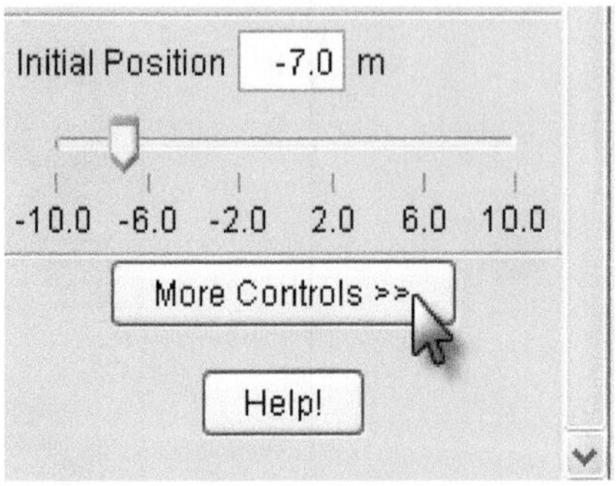 **Figure 3-4** 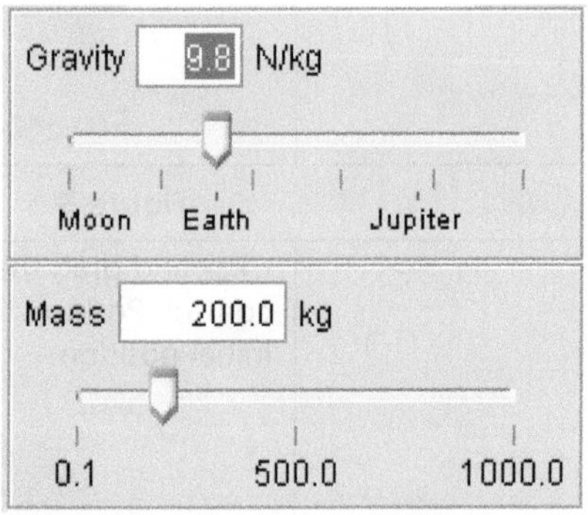 **Figure 3-5**

INTRODUCTION

In everyday language, we use the word force to mean a push or pull. Force is the motivator of motion, the prime mover, so to speak. Newton's second law defines net force as:

$$F = ma$$

where F is the net force, m is the mass, and a is the acceleration of the object.

Changes in an object's motion require the net forces acting on it to be non-zero. Through the free body diagram, an accurate picture can be drawn of how all the forces acting on an object affect it.

In this lab, you will apply Newton's second law to various objects and see the effects of force on the motion of those objects. You will create free body diagrams and calculate the forces acting on the objects.

PROCEDURES

Part 1

1. Apply the following settings for the simulation:

   a. Maximize the screen.
   b. Turn **on** the velocity, position, acceleration, and force graphs.
   c. Turn **off** the friction.
   d. Check F_{Total}
   e. Uncheck $F_{Friction}$
   f. Uncheck $F_{Applied}$
   g. Select the file cabinet for the object.
   h. Slide the position control to **−8m**.
   i. Turn **on** the Free Body Diagram.

   If you have correctly applied the settings, your screen will look similar to Figure 3-6.

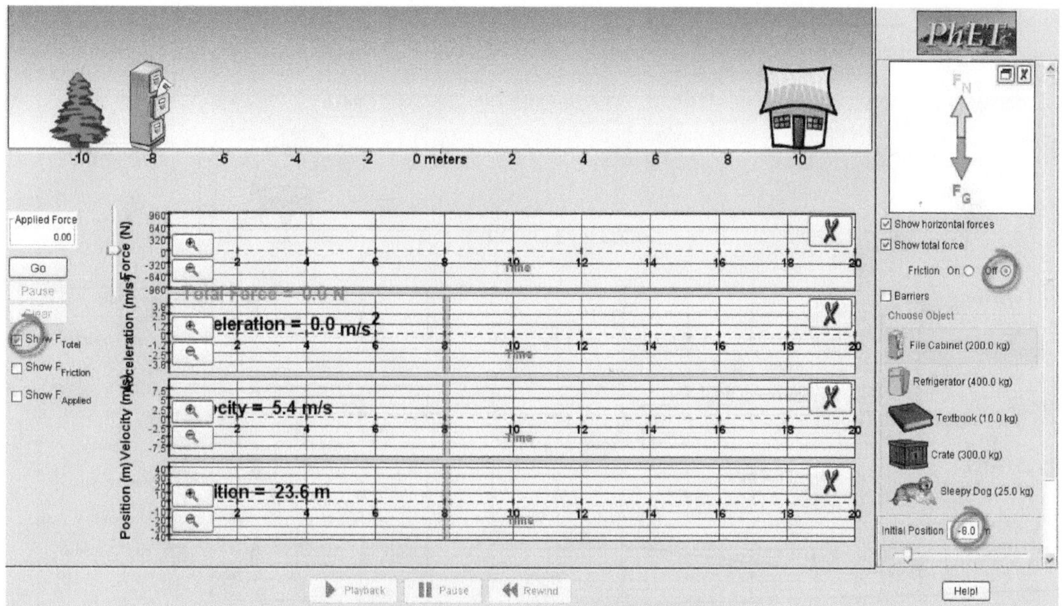

Figure 3-6

2. Apply a force by depressing and holding down the left mouse button while dragging the cursor to the right of the object. Release the button after 4 seconds. Four seconds after releasing the button, click the pause button. Your screen will look similar (but not identical) to Figure 3-7.
3. Draw graphs for acceleration and force using the data from the respective graphs generated by the simulation. Use the graph paper provided at the end of this lab.
4. Use the graphs you completed in the previous step to answer the following questions, using the time interval from 2 to 4 seconds:

   a. What type of curves—linear or parabolic—do you see in each of the graphs?

      i. Acceleration vs. Time : _________

      ii. Force vs. Time: _________

   b. Describe the acceleration in comparison with the force, over the same time frames.

   c. Calculate the force of the object at $t = 3s$. Use the formula $F = ma$. The mass can be found next to the image in the selector panel.

      $F =$ ________ N

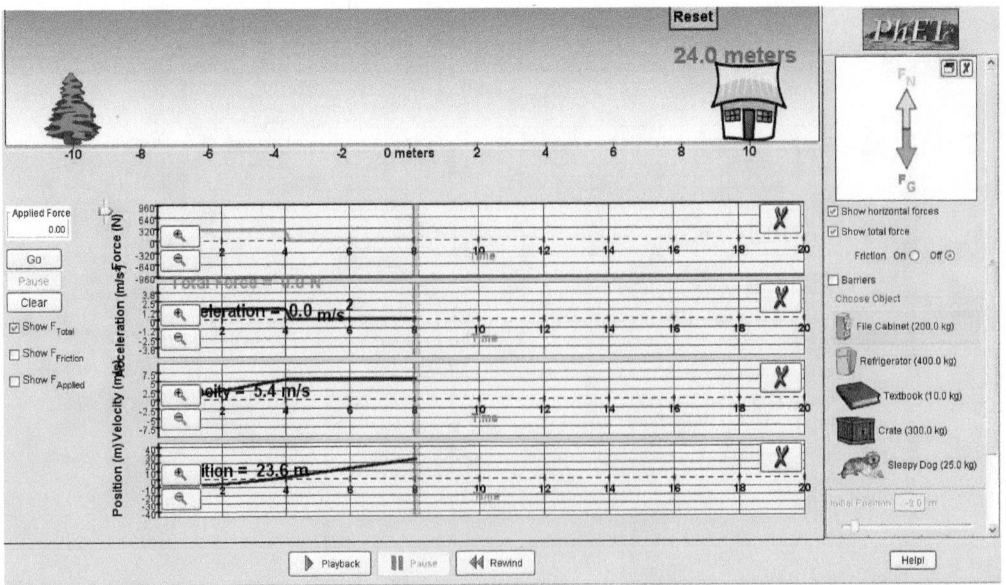

Figure 3-7

d. Use your graph of Force vs. Time to find the force at $t = 3\text{s}$.

$F =$ ________ N

e. Draw the free body diagram for $t = 3\text{s}$ in the space provided below.

5. Click the clear button and apply the following settings:

a. Check F_{Total}
b. Check $F_{Friction}$
c. Check $F_{Applied}$
d. Turn on Friction
e. Set the object's starting position to **−8m**.

Your screen should look similar to Figure 3-6.

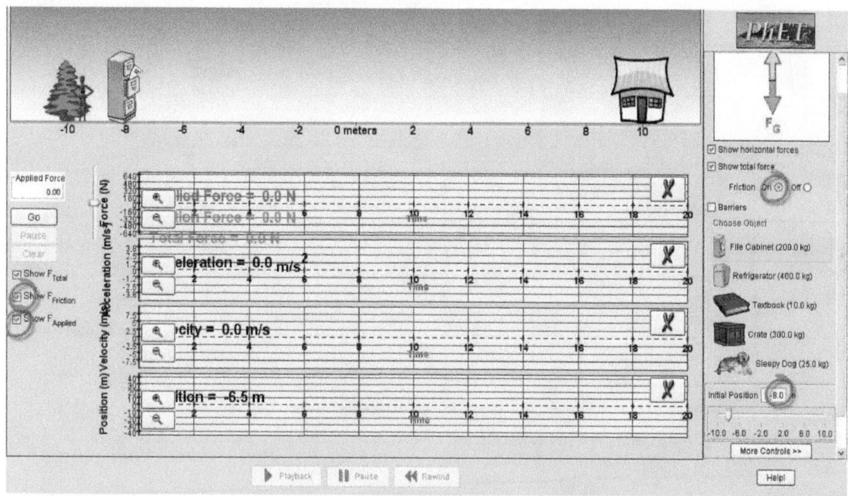

Figure 3-8

6. Start the motion over by applying the force to the right of the object. Keep increasing the force until the object moves. Don't release the mouse button until a total of 5 seconds have passed. After 5 more seconds, click the pause button. Your screen should look similar to Figure 3-9.
7. Draw graphs for acceleration and force using the data from the respective graphs generated by the simulation. Use the graph paper provided at the end of this lab.
8. Use the graphs you completed in the previous step to answer the following questions, using the time interval from 2 to 4 seconds:

   a. What type of curves—linear or parabolic—do you see in each of the graphs?

      i. Acceleration vs. Time: __________
      ii. Force vs. Time: __________

   b. In the interval from 2 to 4 seconds, order the forces—total, applied, and friction—from greatest to smallest.

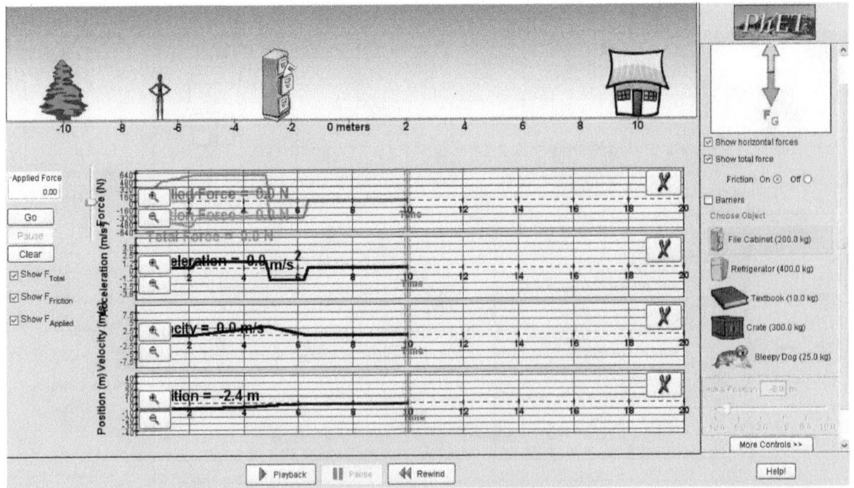

Figure 3-9

c. What relationship does the total force have to the other two forces—applied and friction?

d. Describe the acceleration in comparison with the forces, over the same time frames

e. Calculate the force of the object at $t = 3s$. Use the formula $F = ma$.

$F =$ ________ N

f. Use your graph of Force vs. Time to find the force at $t = 3s$.

$F =$ ________ N

g. Draw the free body diagram for $t = 3s$ in the space provided below.

Part 2

1. Apply the following settings for the simulation:

   a. Maximize the screen.
   b. Turn **on** the velocity, position, acceleration, and force graphs.
   c. Turn **off** the friction.
   d. Check F_{Total}
   e. Uncheck $F_{Friction}$
   f. Uncheck $F_{Applied}$
   g. Select a different object other than the file cabinet, the example Figure 3-10 depicts the selection of the refrigerator as the object.
   h. Slide the position control to **−8m**.
   i. Turn **on** the Free Body Diagram.

   If you have correctly applied the settings your screen will look similar to Figure 3-10.

2. Apply a force by depressing and holding down the left mouse button while dragging the cursor to the right of the object. Release the button after 4 seconds. Four seconds after releasing the button, click the pause button. Your screen will look similar (but not identical) to Figure 3-11.

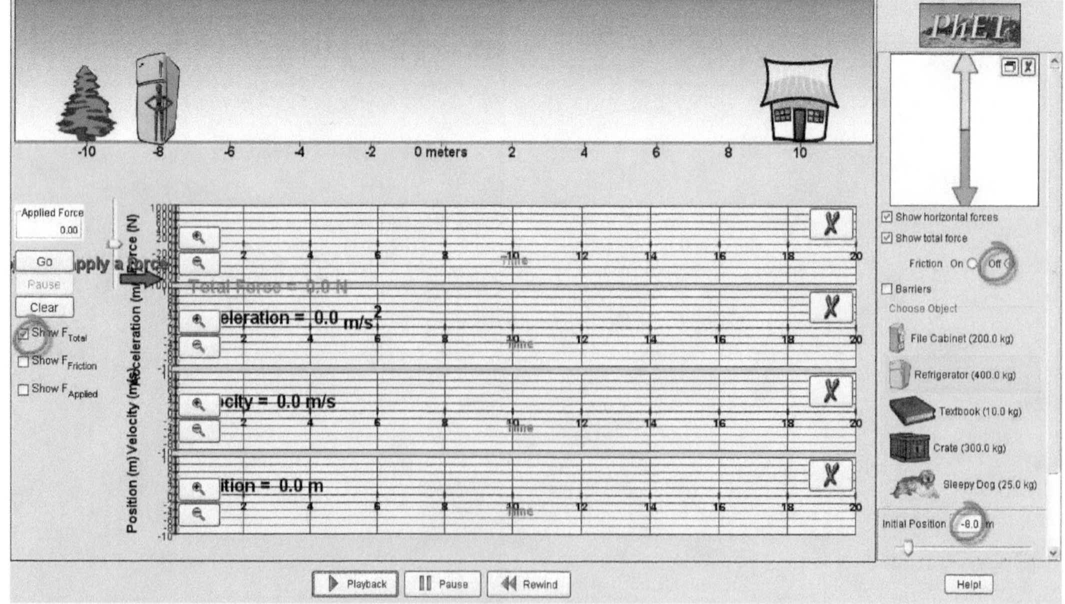

Figure 3-10

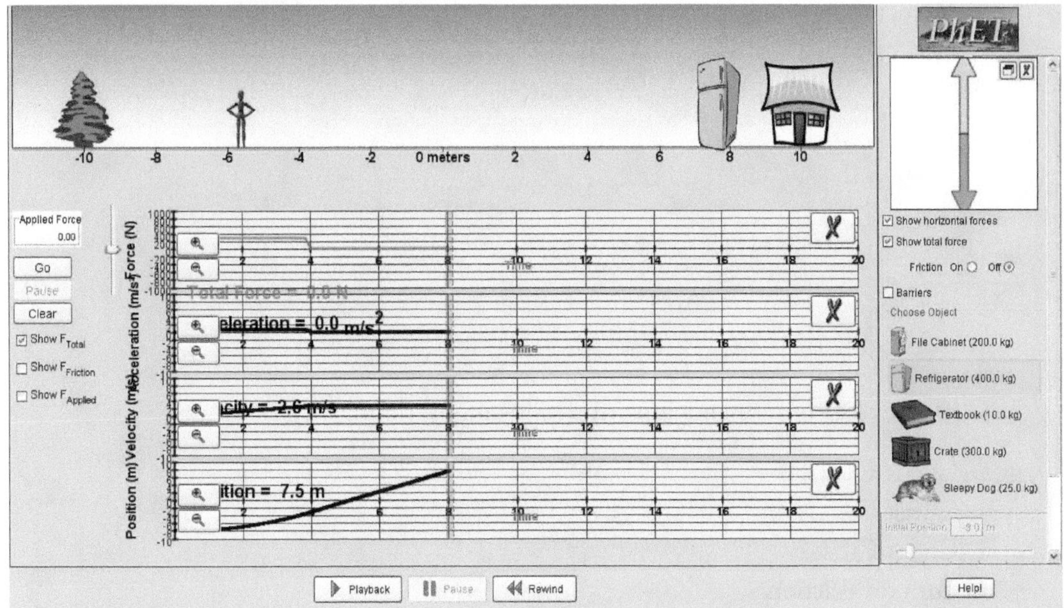

Figure 3-11

3. Draw graphs for acceleration and force using the data collected from the respective graphs generated by the simulation. Use the graph paper provided at the end of this lab.
4. Use the graphs you completed in the previous step to answer the following questions using the time interval from 2 to 4 seconds:

   a. What type of curves—linear or parabolic—do you see in each of the graphs?

      i. Acceleration vs. Time: __________
      ii. Force vs. Time: __________

   b. Describe the acceleration in comparison with the force, over the same time frames.

   c. Calculate the force of the object at $t = 3s$. Use the formula.

      $F =$ _________ N

   d. Use your graph of Force vs. Time to find the force at $t = 3s$.

      $F =$ _________ N

e. Draw the free body diagram for $t = 3s$ in the space provided below.

5. Click the clear button and apply the following settings:

   a. Check F_{Total}
   b. Check $F_{Friction}$
   c. Check $F_{Applied}$
   d. Turn on Friction
   e. Select a different object other than the file cabinet or the refrigerator. The example in Figure 3-12 uses the dog as the object.
   f. Set the object's starting position to **−8m**.

   Your screen should look similar to Figure 3-12.

6. Start the motion over by applying the force to the right of the object. Keep increasing the force until the object moves. Don't release the mouse button until a total of 5 seconds have passed. After 5 more seconds, click the pause button. Your screen should look similar to Figure 3-13.

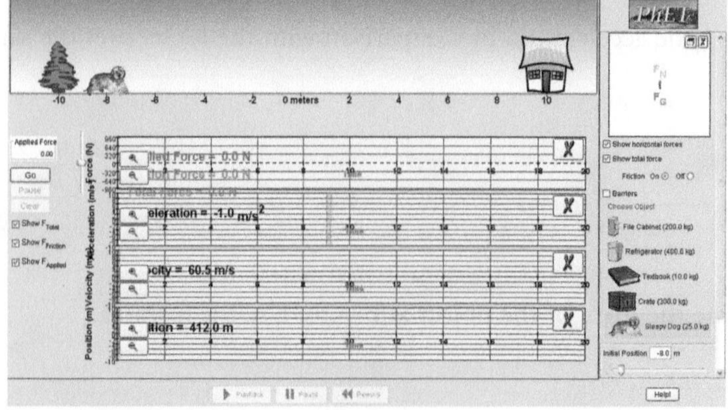

Figure 3-12

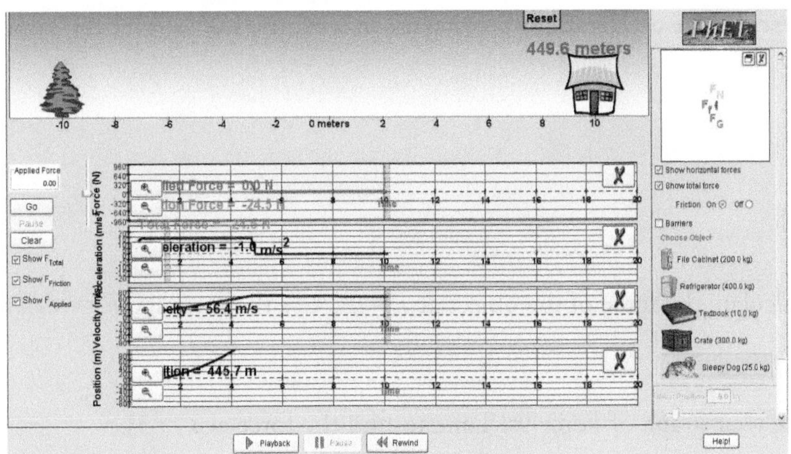

Figure 3-13

7. Draw graphs for acceleration and force using the data from the respective graphs generated by the simulation. Use the graph paper provided at the end of this lab.
8. Use the graphs you completed in the previous step to answer the following questions, using the time interval from 2 to 4 seconds:

   a. What type of curves—linear or parabolic—do you see in each of the graphs?

      i. Acceleration vs. Time: __________
      ii. Force vs. Time: __________

   b. In the interval from 2 to 4 seconds, order the forces—total, applied, and friction—from greatest to smallest.

   c. What relationship does the total force have to the other two forces—applied and friction?

d. Describe the acceleration in comparison with the forces, over the same time frames.

e. Calculate the force of the object at $t = 3s$. Use the formula $F = ma$.

$F =$ ________ N

f. Use your graph of Force vs. Time to find the force at $t = 3s$.

$F =$ ________ N

g. Draw the free body diagram in the space provided below.

QUESTIONS

1. Did you see any differences, in the graphs between the two different objects?

2. How did your calculated values for the force compare to the graph values?

3. Is it possible to have negative values for any of the variables of force, position, velocity and acceleration (at any time)? If so, describe the motion that could create these values.

4. How do the graphs change when friction is turned on?

Part 1 Step 3 Graphs

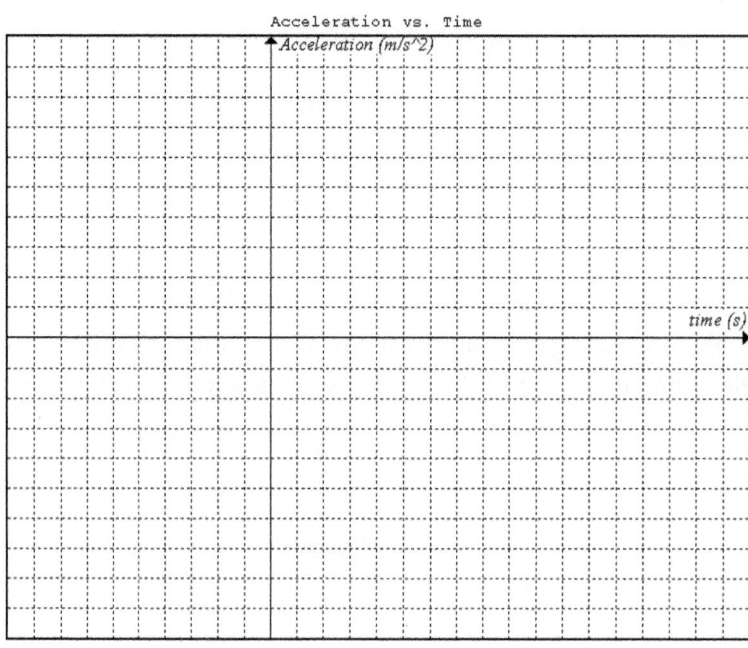

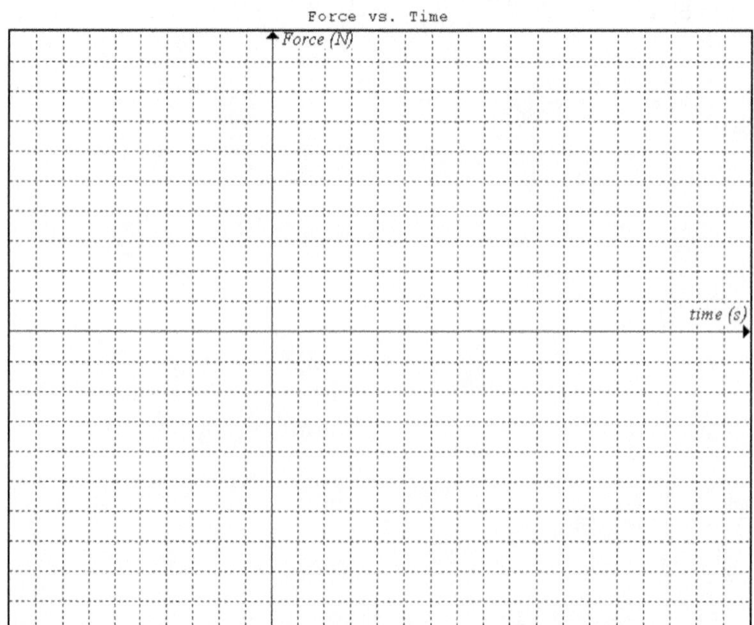

Part 1 Step 7 Graphs

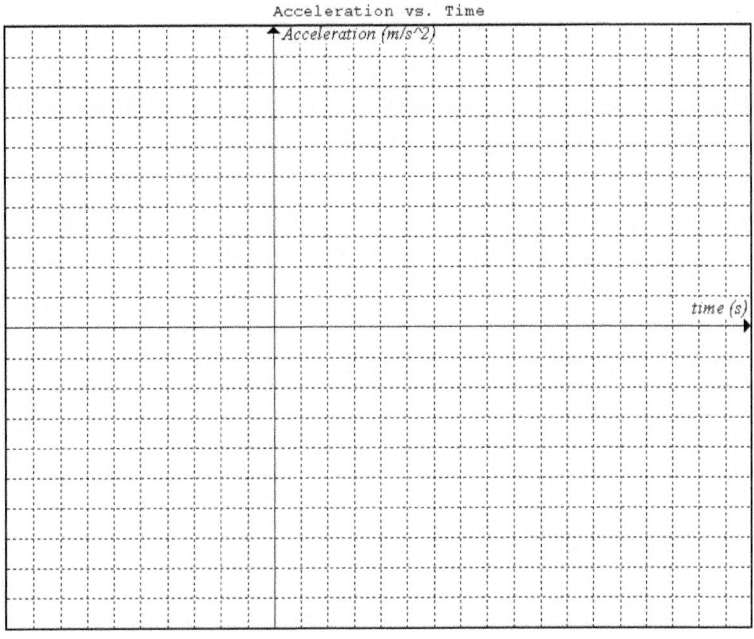

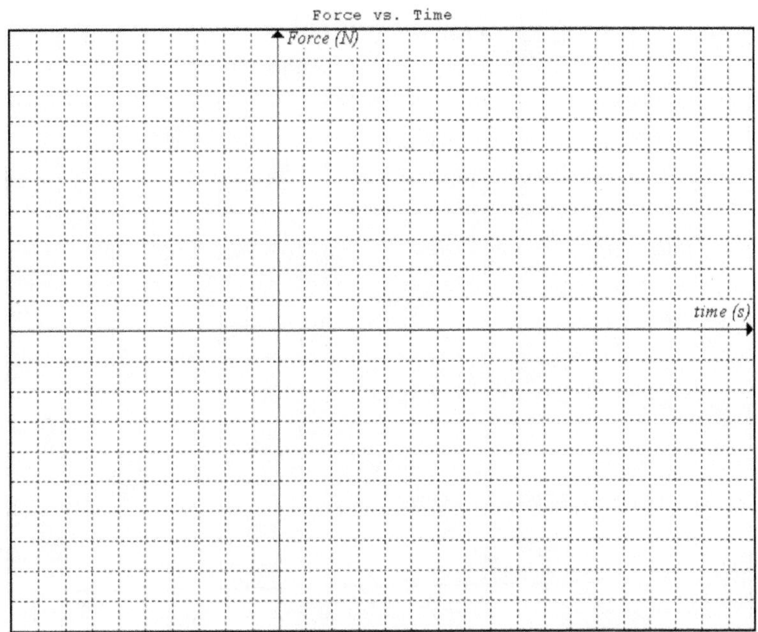

Part 2 Step 3 Graphs

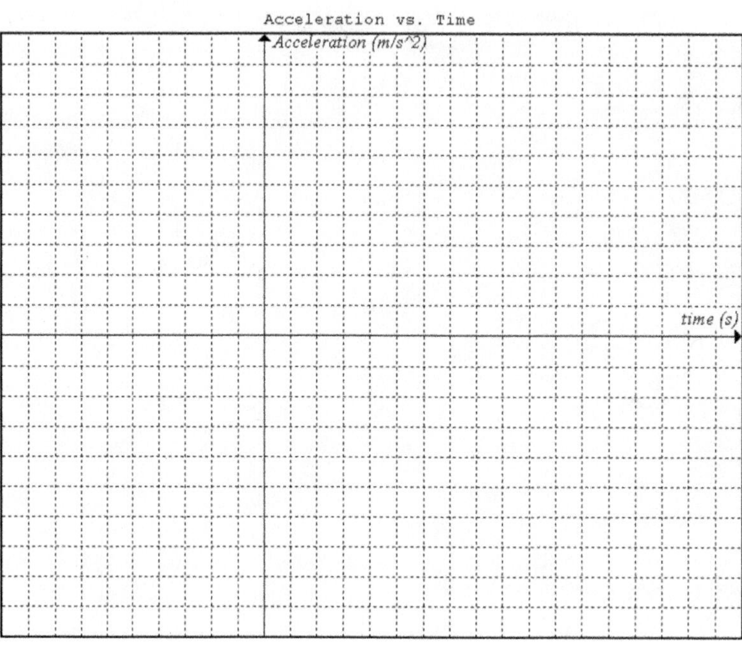

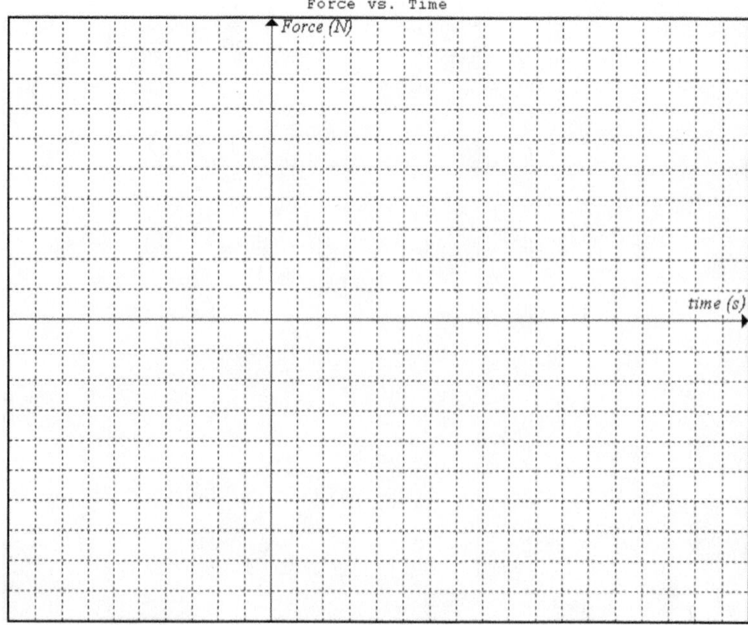

Part 2 Step 7 Graphs

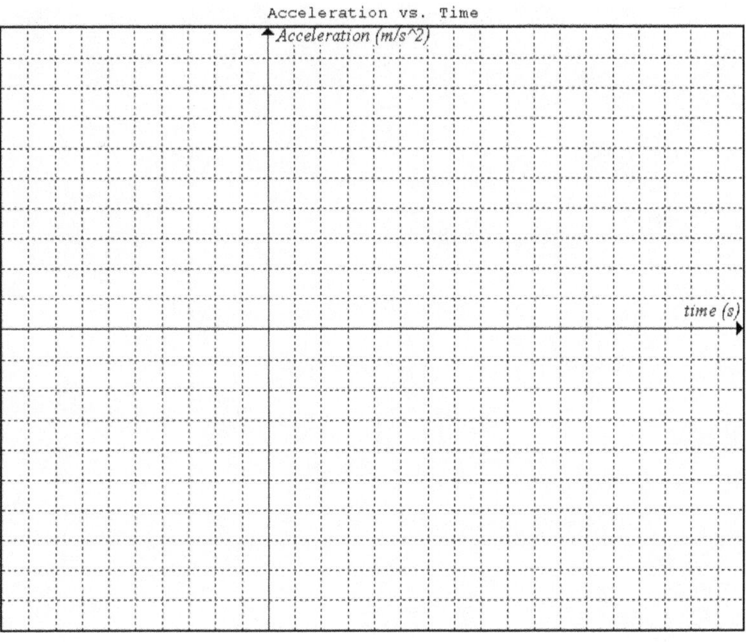

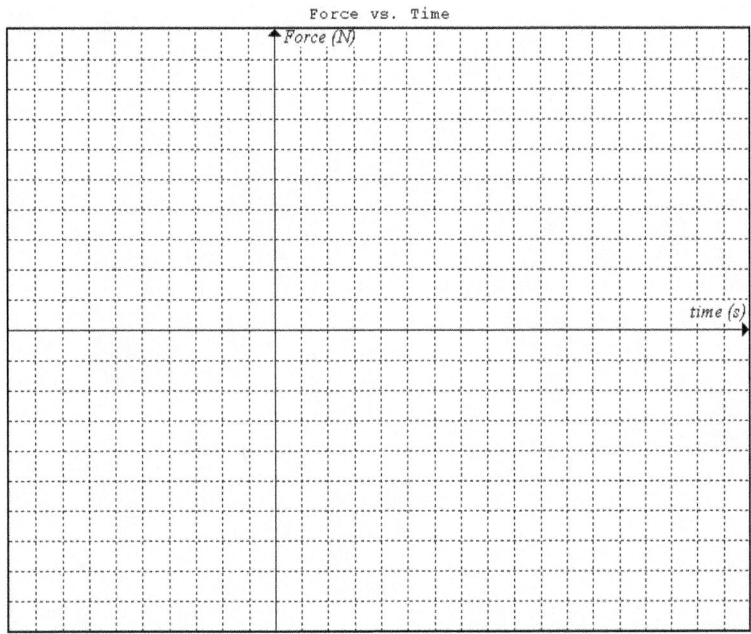

4

ENERGY

PURPOSE

The purpose of this lab is to investigate energy and how it is applied to motion.

SIMULATIONS

Energy Skate Park

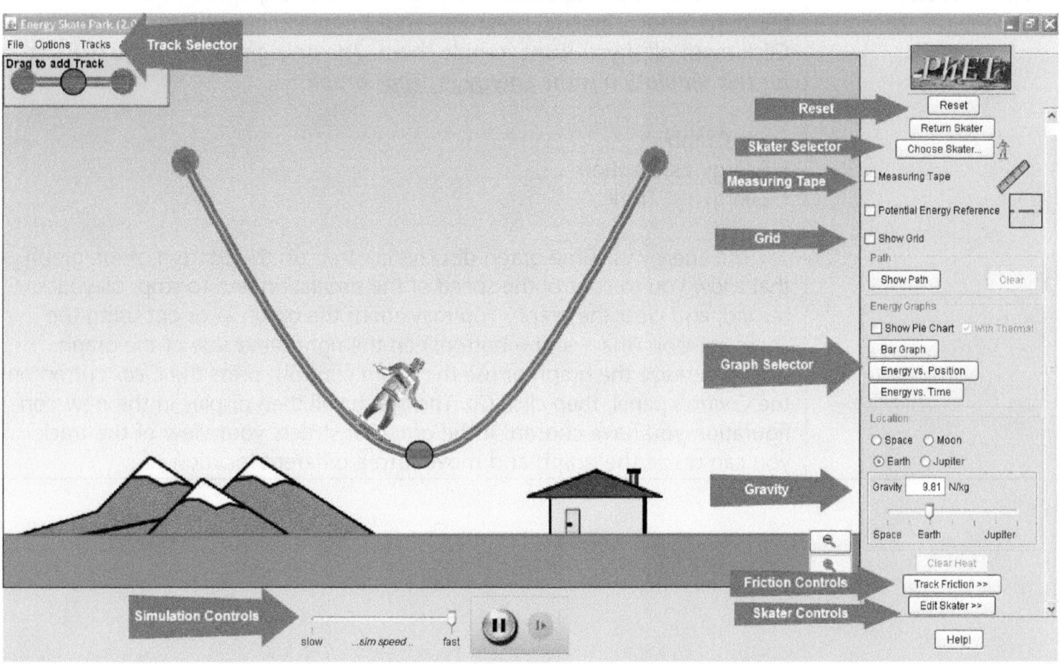

Figure 4-1

Feature	Control
Figure 4-1	
Track Selector	Click on the Track selector and pick one of the following track types: • Loop • Double Well • Double Well (Roller Coaster) • Friction Parabola • Jump • S-Curve • Fly Off (bug)
Reset	This resets the simulation to default values and sets the track to Friction Parabola track.
Skater Selector	Clicking on *Choose Skater* will allow you to choose a skateboarder with a different mass.
Measuring Tape	Check the *Measuring Tape* box when you want to make measurements. A tape measure appears on the screen, which you can manipulate within the simulation.
Grid	Check *Show Grid* if you want grid lines to appear on the screen. This will make it easier for you to estimate measurements.
Graph Selector	Click on the following buttons if you would like a graph that depicts relationships among kinetic, potential, and thermal energy of the simulation. Click them off if you want to hide them. ***The only graph that you will use for this simulation is the <u>Energy vs. Time</u> graph.*** • Bar Graph • Energy vs. Position • Energy vs. Time The Energy vs. Time graph displays controls on the bottom of the graph that allow you to control the speed of the simulation and to stop, playback, rewind, and clear the graph. You may zoom the graph in or out using the zoom controls (the + and – buttons) on the right-hand side of the graph. After you resize the graph or use the zoom controls, press the *Clear* button on the *Controls* panel, then click *Go*. The graph will then display in the new configuration you have chosen. If the graph obstructs your view of the track, you can resize the graph and move it to a different location.

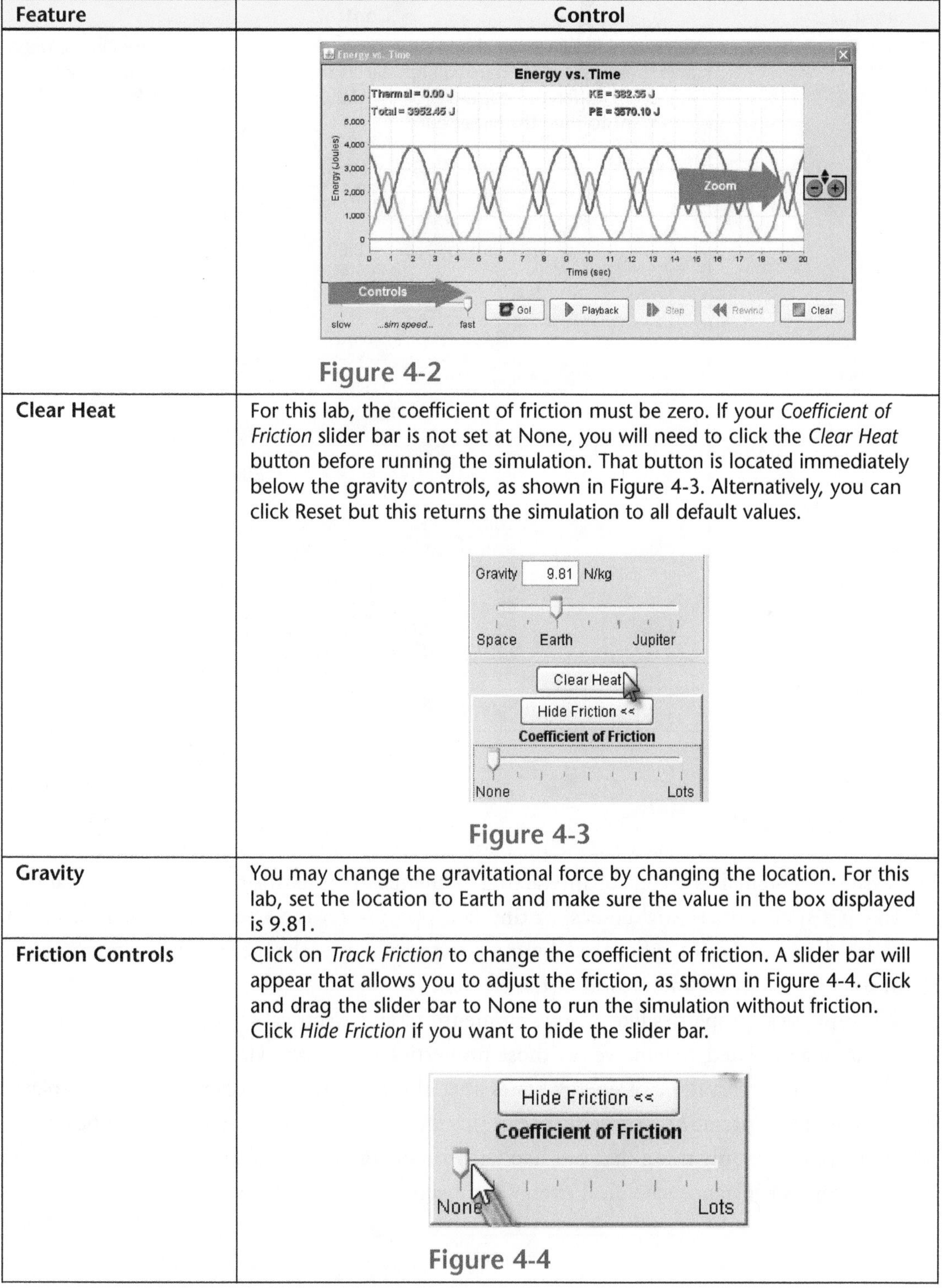

Feature	Control
	Figure 4-2
Clear Heat	For this lab, the coefficient of friction must be zero. If your *Coefficient of Friction* slider bar is not set at None, you will need to click the *Clear Heat* button before running the simulation. That button is located immediately below the gravity controls, as shown in Figure 4-3. Alternatively, you can click Reset but this returns the simulation to all default values. Figure 4-3
Gravity	You may change the gravitational force by changing the location. For this lab, set the location to Earth and make sure the value in the box displayed is 9.81.
Friction Controls	Click on *Track Friction* to change the coefficient of friction. A slider bar will appear that allows you to adjust the friction, as shown in Figure 4-4. Click and drag the slider bar to None to run the simulation without friction. Click *Hide Friction* if you want to hide the slider bar. Figure 4-4

Continues

Feature	Control
Skater Controls	Click on Edit Skater to change the properties of the skater: bounciness, mass, and stickiness. Slider bars will appear as shown in Figure 4-5 that let you adjust the different properties of the skater. Click Hide Skater Properties if you want to hide the slider bars. 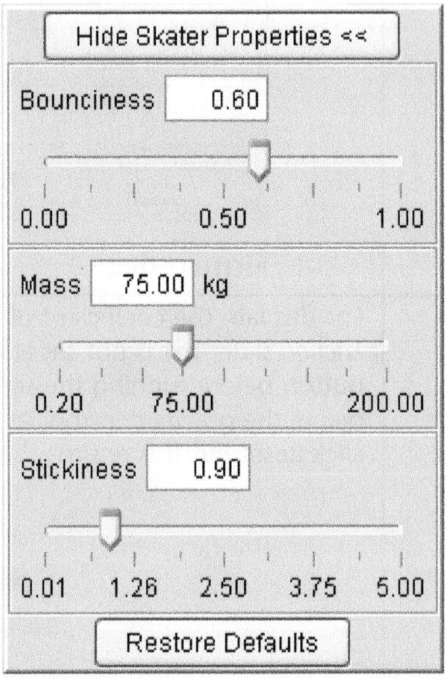 Hide Skater Properties << Bounciness 0.60 0.00 0.50 1.00 Mass 75.00 kg 0.20 75.00 200.00 Stickiness 0.90 0.01 1.26 2.50 3.75 5.00 Restore Defaults **Figure 4-5**

INTRODUCTION

In physics, a system is a group of interacting elements. A system can be huge (for example, a galaxy is a system of celestial bodies) or tiny (a drop of water is a system of water molecules). An isolated system is not influenced by outside forces—any changes in the elements come about solely through the interaction of the elements.

When physical properties like energy, momentum, and electrical charge remain unchanged over time in an isolated system, we say those properties are conserved.

The law of conservation of energy states that the total amount of energy in an isolated system remains constant. As a consequence of this law, we can say that energy cannot be created nor destroyed. The only thing that can happen with energy in an isolated system is that it can change form. For instance, chemical energy can become thermal energy.

In mechanics, conservation of energy is usually stated as conservation of the total mechanical energy. Total mechanical energy is the sum of an object's kinetic energy and its potential energy:

$$E = K.E. + P.E.$$

where E is the total mechanical energy, $K.E.$ is the kinetic energy, and $P.E.$ is the potential energy

We can calculate the kinetic and potential energy of an object using these equations:

$$K.E. = \frac{1}{2}mv^2$$

where m is mass and v is velocity

$$P.E. = mgh$$

where m is mass in kilograms, g is gravitational acceleration in m/s^2, and h is height in meters

A conservative system is one in which no energy is dissipated. Therefore, the total mechanical energy remains constant. Work (which is the transfer of energy) done by a force in a conservative system is independent of path and completely reversible. For example, the force required to change the potential energy of the object by moving it does not depend on the path taken. The potential energy is also completely reversible—just move the object back.

Contrast a conservative system with a system involving friction—the work done to get between states *does* depend on the path taken and is *not* reversible. Systems that involve friction are examples of open dissipative systems operating far from thermodynamic equilibrium in an environment where they exchange energy and matter.

In this lab, you will investigate these concepts by measuring the energy of objects as they move in a gravitational field in an isolated system with both conservative and non-conservative forces at work.

PROCEDURES

Part 1: Friction Parabola Track

1. Apply the following settings for the simulation:

   a. Maximize the screen.
   b. Click *Reset.*
   c. Set the track type to **Friction Parabola.**
   d. Set gravity to 9.81 by selecting the location as Earth.
   e. Use the friction control to set the Coefficient of Friction to **None.**

   If you have correctly applied the settings, your screen will look similar to Figure 4-6.

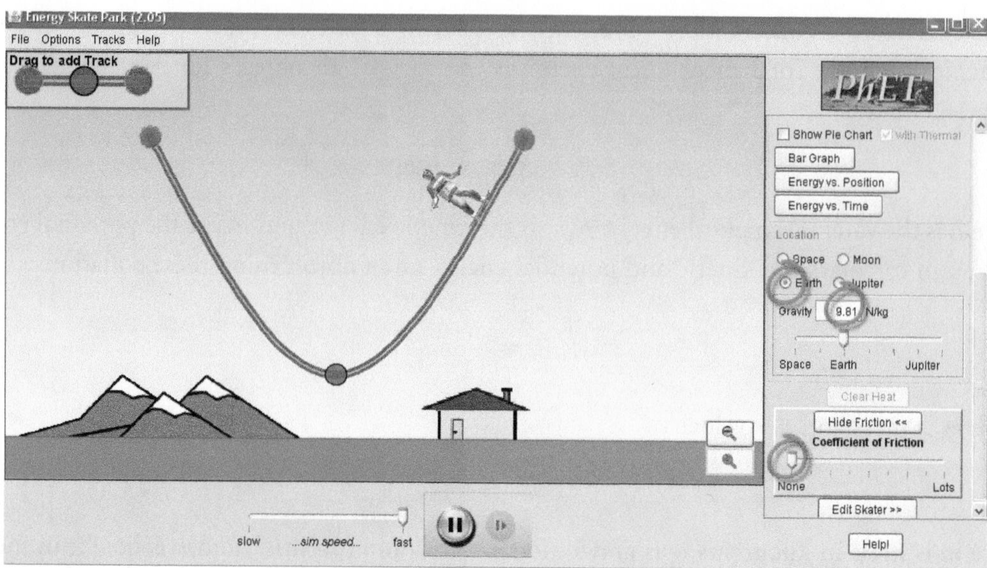

Figure 4-6

2. Click on the Energy vs. Time graph. Your screen should look similar to Figure 4-7.
3. Where is the skateboarder located on the track when his kinetic energy is the:

   a. highest? ____________
   b. lowest? ____________

   Tip: If you're having trouble watching the skateboarder and the graph moving simultaneously, use the … sim speed … slider control at the bottom of the window to slow down the animation.

4. Where is the skateboarder located on the track when his potential energy is the:

   a. highest? ____________
   b. lowest? ____________

5. Where is the skateboarder located on the track when his total energy is the:

   a. highest? ____________
   b. lowest? ____________

6. What is the value of the thermal energy in this situation? Why?

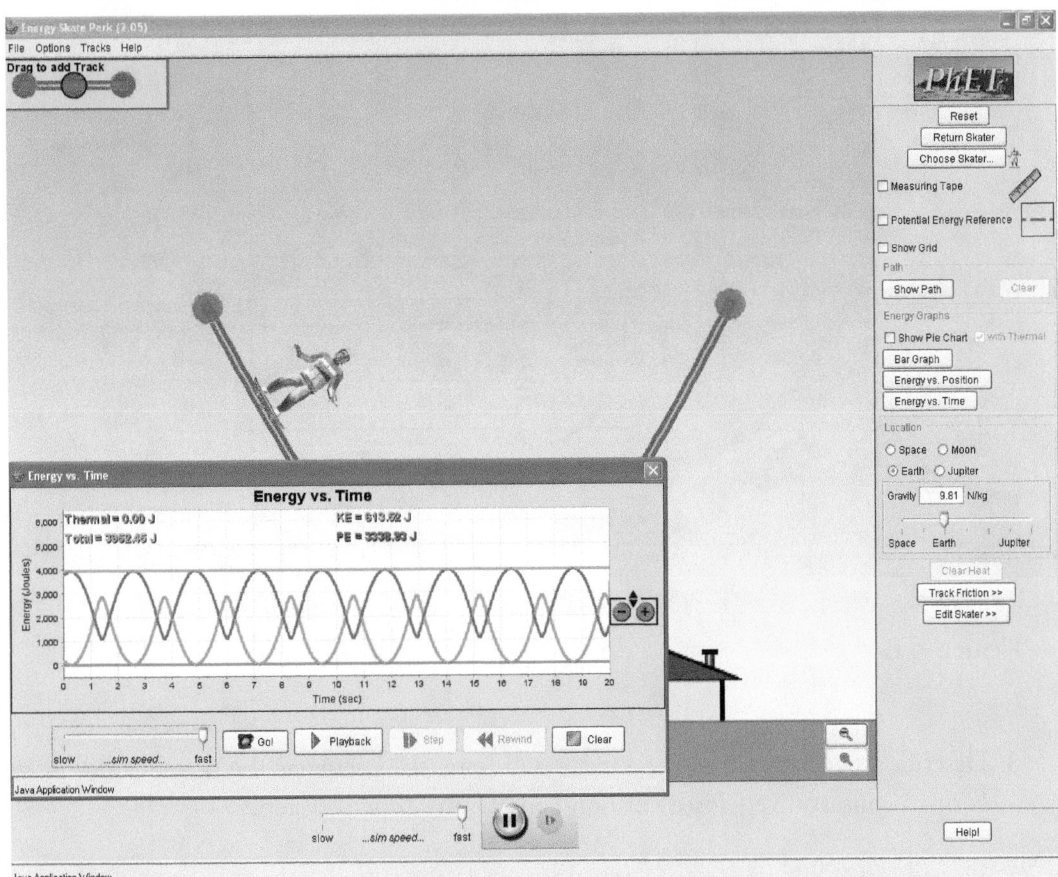

Figure 4-7

Part 1: Loop Track

7. Apply the following settings for the simulation:

   a. Maximize the screen.
   b. Set the track type to **Loop**.
   c. Set gravity to 9.81 by selecting the location as Earth.
   d. Use the fiction control to set the Coefficient of Friction to **None**.
   e. Check the Measuring Tape box.
   f. Check the Potential Energy Reference box.
   g. If the *Clear Heat* button is enabled, click it.
   h. If your skater properties are visible, click the Hide Skater Properties button.
   i. Click on the Energy vs. Time graph.

If you have correctly applied the settings, your screen will look similar to Figure 4-8.

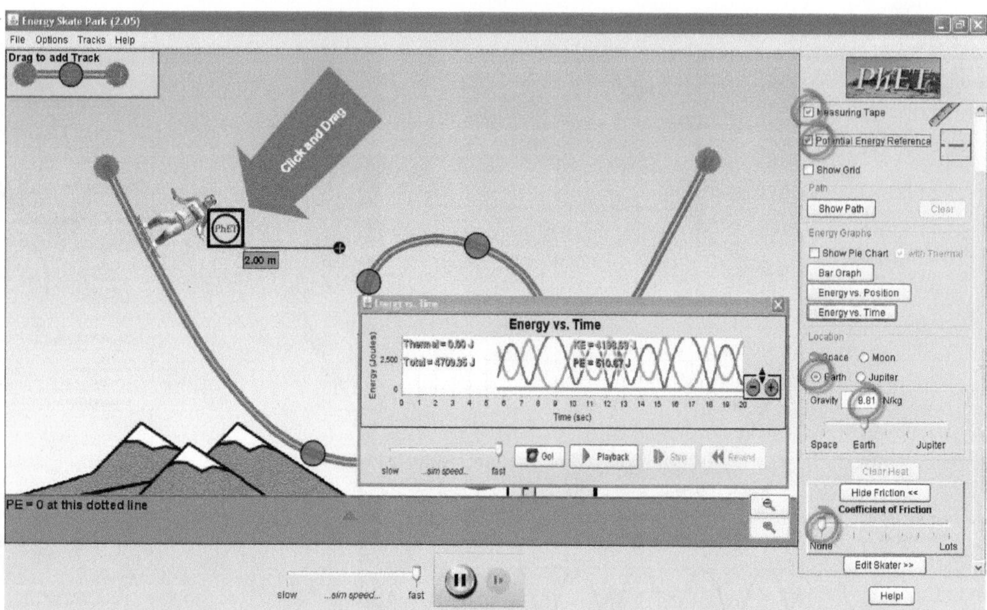

Figure 4-8

8. Describe what happens to the kinetic and potential energy as the skateboarder moves. Is this a conservative (closed) or non-conservative (open) system?

9. What is the maximum potential energy for this motion? Where is the skateboarder located on the track when he reaches that energy?

10. Use the tape measure to find the height where the skater's potential energy is the greatest. To get an accurate measurement, you need to align the cross hair on the end of the tape measure with the skater's center of mass. The center of mass is the red dot on the bottom of the skateboard. Measure the height of the highest point the skateboarder reaches on the loop. Your measurement will appear in the green box next to the tape measure, as shown in Figure 4-9.

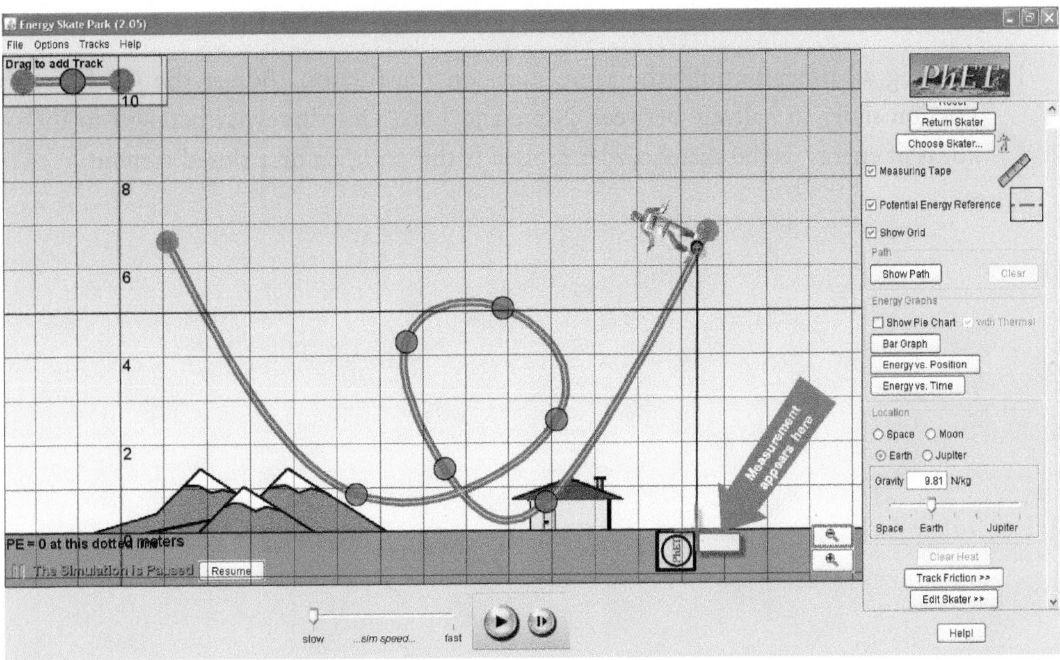

Figure 4-9

11. Use the formula for potential energy to find the mass of the skateboarder. Your answer should be in kilograms.

    Potential Energy $= mgh$

12. Click the Edit Skater >> button. Compare your answer to the actual value in the Mass window.

    Calculated mass = ____________

    Actual mass = ____________

Part 1: Add Friction

13. Keeping all other settings the same, turn on the friction. Adjust the Coefficient of Friction slider to halfway between None and Lots. Describe what happens to the two kinds of energy as the skateboarder moves. Is this an open or a closed system?

Part 2: Friction Parabola Track

1. Apply the following settings for the simulation:
    a. Maximize the screen.
    b. Click Reset.
    c. Set the track type to **Friction Parabola.**
    d. Use the *Select a Skater* button to select a different rider than in Part 1 of this lab.
    e. Set gravity to 9.81 by selecting the location as Earth.
    f. Use the friction control to set the coefficient to **None**.
    g. Click on the Energy vs. Time graph.
2. Where is your new skateboarder located on the track when the kinetic energy is the:
    a. highest?
    b. lowest?
3. Where is your new skateboarder located on the track when the potential energy is the:
    a. highest?
    b. lowest?
4. Where is your new skateboarder located on the track when the total energy is the:
    a. highest?
    b. lowest?

5. What is the value of the thermal energy in this situation? Why?

Part 2: Loop Track

6. Apply the following settings for the simulation:
   a. Maximize the screen.
   b. Click *Reset.*
   c. Set the track type to **Loop**.
   d. Set gravity to 9.81 by selecting the location as Earth.
   e. Use the friction control to set the coefficient to **None**.
   f. Check the Measuring Tape box.
   g. Check the Potential Energy Reference box.
   h. Click on the Energy vs. Time graph.
7. Describe what happens to the two kinds of energy as the skateboarder moves.

8. What is the maximum potential energy for this motion? Where is the location of the skateboarder on the track for that energy?

9. Use the tape measure to measure the height of the skateboard where potential energy is the greatest, as you did in Part 1.

10. Find the mass of the skateboarder using the formula for potential energy:

    $P.E. = mgh$

11. Click the Edit Skater >> button and compare your answer with the actual value.

    Calculated mass = ___________

    Actual mass = ___________

12. Turn on the friction. Adjust the *Coefficient of Friction* so the slider bar is half way between *None* and *Lots*. Describe what happens to the two kinds of energy and the total energy as the skateboarder moves.

QUESTIONS

1. Did you see any differences in the graphs between the two different objects?

2. How did your calculated values for the mass compare to the actual values?

3. How did kinetic energy and potential energy compare to the total energy during the motion without friction? What about when friction was turned on?

5

TWO-DIMENSIONAL MOTION

PURPOSE

The purpose of this lab is to investigate two-dimensional motion.

SIMULATIONS

Projectile Motion

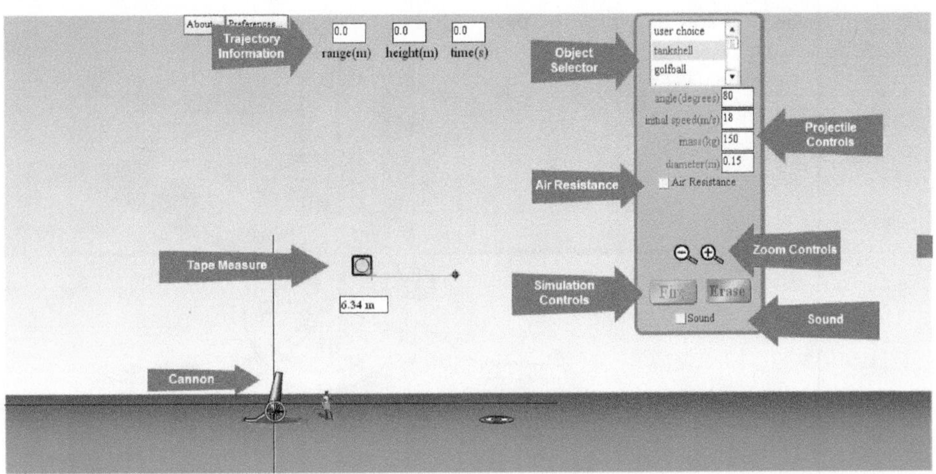

Figure 5-1

Feature	Control
	Figure 5-1
Trajectory Information	As the projectile travels along its path, these boxes will show the range, height of the object at that point in time.
Tape Measure	To move the tape measure, click and drag it to the location of your choice. Elongate the tape by clicking and dragging on the end of the tape as shown in Figure 5-2.  Figure 5-2
Cannon	Then angle of the cannon can be changed by clicking on the barrel and dragging it to the desired angle. The position of the cannon can be changed by clicking and dragging the base of the cannon. 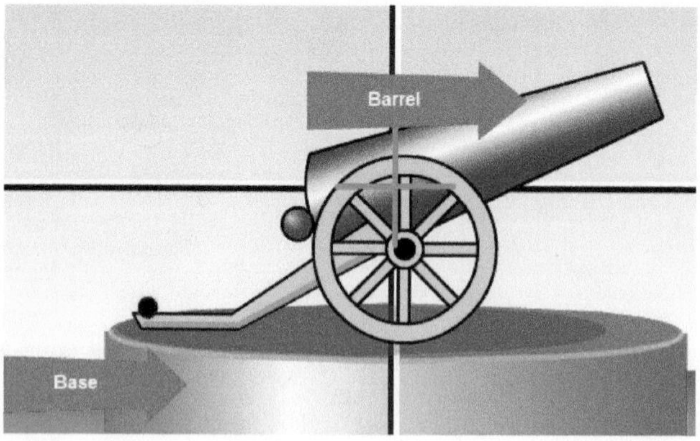 Figure 5-3
Object Selector	You can pick different objects to shoot out of the cannon by using the Object Selector. Drag the scroll bar up and down to view all of the different objects. Click on the object you want to use.
Projectile Controls	You can manually change the following settings by typing values into the respective boxes: • Angle • initial speed • mass • diameter

Feature	Control
Air Resistance	To add air resistance, check the Air Resistance box.
Zoom Controls	The magnify glasses can be used to zoom in or out.
Simulation Controls	Click the *Fire* button to launch an object. The simulation is designed so you can change the angle and show more than one path at a time. When you want to clear the screen, click the *Erase* button.
Sound	To add sound to the simulation, check the Sound box.

INTRODUCTION

Kinematics deals with the concepts of motion, things like velocity, position, and acceleration. By using kinematic formulas, we can mathematically model and predict motion.

Here are the basic two-dimensional kinematic formulas:

$$v_x = v_{0x} + a_x t$$
$$v_y = v_{0y} + a_y t$$
$$x - x_0 = v_{0x} t + \frac{1}{2} a_x t^2$$
$$y - y_0 = v_{0y} t + \frac{1}{2} a_y t^2$$
$$v_x^2 = v_{0x}^2 + 2a_x x$$
$$v_y^2 = v_{0y}^2 + 2a_y y$$

For these equations, we assume that the acceleration is constant and the initial time is set to zero.

$$\vec{v} = (v_x v_y) \vec{a} = (a_x a_y)$$

Quantities such as displacement, velocity, and acceleration are vector quantities. Vectors are an essential part of describing motion. Vectors have both a magnitude (length) and a direction (angle, measured counter-clockwise from the positive part of the x-axis). As a result, in the rectangular coordinate system, vectors have both horizontal and vertical components.

The horizontal component for velocity is $v = v cos\theta$ and the vertical component is $v = v sin\theta$.

The following equation for the magnitude of velocity results by applying the Pythagorean Theorem:

$$v = \sqrt{v_x^2 + v_y^2}$$

The following kinematic equations relate vector quantities:

$$\text{Velocity: } \vec{v} = (v_x v_y)$$

$$\text{Acceleration: } \vec{a} = (a_x a_y)$$

When working with projectiles, we apply these kinematic equations with the following specifications:

$\vec{v}_0 = (v_0, \theta)$ The vector of initial velocity has the magnitude v_0 and angle θ (the angle of launch).
$a_x = 0$ There is no acceleration in the horizontal direction.
$a_y = -g$ Gravitational acceleration is directed downwards.

When the kinematic equations are applied with the given specifications, other useful equations can be derived.

One such equation is the following formula for range—the maximum horizontal displacement of the projectile:

$$R = \frac{v_0^2 sin(2\theta)}{g}$$

Other useful formulas are:

The formula for the maximum height $\quad h = y_{max} - y_0 = \dfrac{v_0^2 \cdot \sin^2\theta}{2g}$

The formula for the total time of flight $\quad t_{total} = \dfrac{2v_0 \cdot \sin\theta}{g}$

In this lab, you will use data from the experiment to solve equations that can be used to predict the motion of the object. You will investigate the relationships between angles and trajectory.

PROCEDURES

Part 1

1. Apply the following settings for the simulation:

   a. Maximize the screen.
   b. Select the **tankshell** using the Object Selector.
   c. On the Projectile Controls panel, set the angle of the cannon to **75 degrees**.
   d. Turn **off** air resistance.
   e. Turn **off** the sound.

   If you have correctly applied the settings, your screen will look similar to Figure 5-4.
2. To launch the tank shell, click the Fire button.

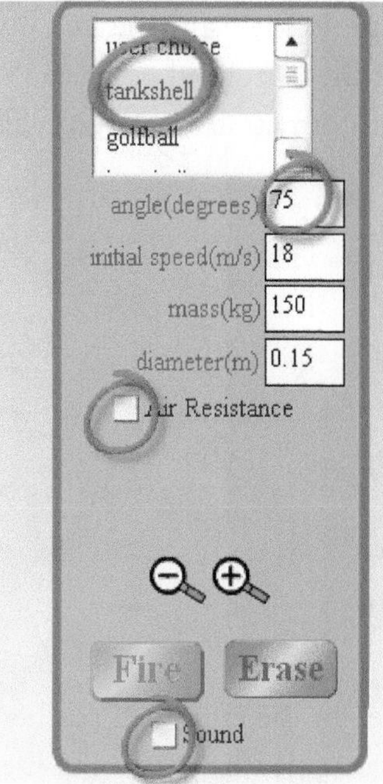

Figure 5-4

3. Use the tape measure to find the height to the top of the arc made by the tank shell. Figure 5-5 shows how to align the tape measure. Record your measurements:

   $h =$ ________

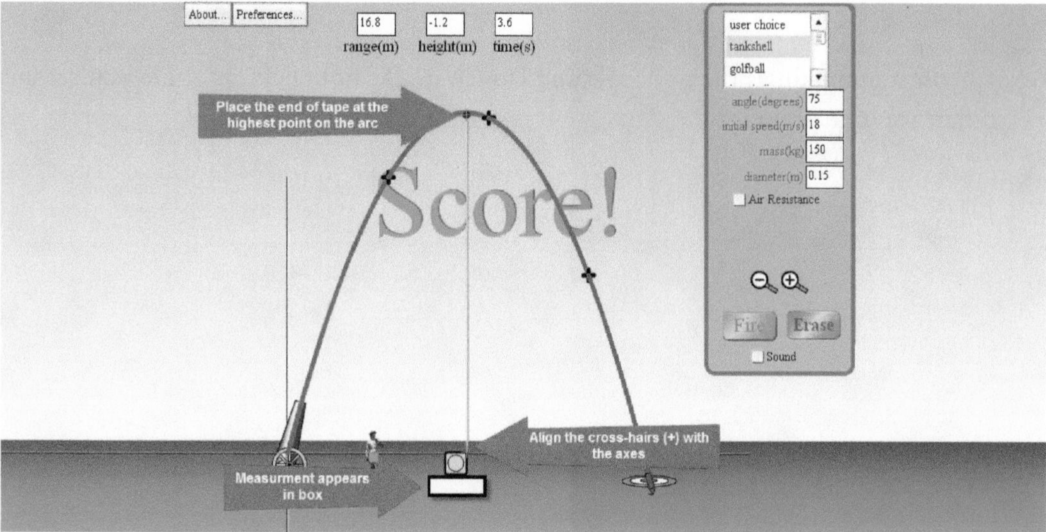

Figure 5-5

4. Calculate the range of the projectile using the initial speed and angle. Use $g = 9.8\frac{m}{s}$ for your calculation. Compare the calculated range to the actual range. The actual range is located in the Trajectory Information range box. Show your work for the calculated range.

   Calculated range = ________

   Actual range = ________

5. Calculate the maximum height the tank shell reaches using the initial speed, half-time, and angle. Compare the calculated height to the measured height from Step 3 of this lab. The initial speed and angle are located in the Projectile Controls panel. To determine the half-time, divide the time located in the Trajectory Information panel by two. Show your work for the calculated height.

   Calculated height =

6. Choose a pumpkin as the projectile and launch it. Do **not** click *Erase.* Do you see any difference in its trajectory?

Part 2: Pumpkin

1. Apply the following settings for the simulation:

   a. Maximize the screen.
   b. Do **not** click the *Erase* button.
   c. Keep the **pumpkin** as the selected object.
   d. Leave the angle of the cannon on **75 degrees**.
   e. Turn **on** air resistance.
   f. Leave the sound turned **off**.

   Click the Fire button to launch the pumpkin.
2. Use the tape measure to find the height to the top of the arc made by the pumpkin. Record your measurements:

   Measured height: ___________ m

3. Calculate the range and the height of the pumpkin as shown in Part 1 of the lab. Compare the calculated and measured values. Show your work for the calculated values.

   Calculated range = ________

   Actual range = ________ Difference between calculated and actual: _______

   Calculated height = ________

   Actual height = ________ Difference between calculated and actual: _______

Part 3: Tank Shell

1. Keep the same settings except choose the tank shell as the object. Do **not** click the *Erase* button.
2. Click the *Fire* button to launch the tank shell.
3. What do you notice about the trajectory of the tank shell with air resistance compared the other trials you performed in this lab?

4. Erase the current screen. Select the tank shell and set the angle to 11° and fire the shell. Now select the pumpkin and set the angle to 12.7° and fire the pumpkin. How do the trajectories compare?

QUESTIONS

1. Did you see any differences in the trajectories between the different objects in both parts of the lab?

2. Show how your calculated values for the tank shell and pumpkin—with air resistance and without air resistance—compare to the actual values.

3. What angle do you need to set the cannon to get the maximum range and height—without air resistance?

6

GAS PROPERTIES

PURPOSE

The purpose of this lab is to investigate how properties of gases—pressure, temperature, and volume—are related. Also, you will investigate the principle of buoyancy.

SIMULATIONS

Balloons and Buoyancy

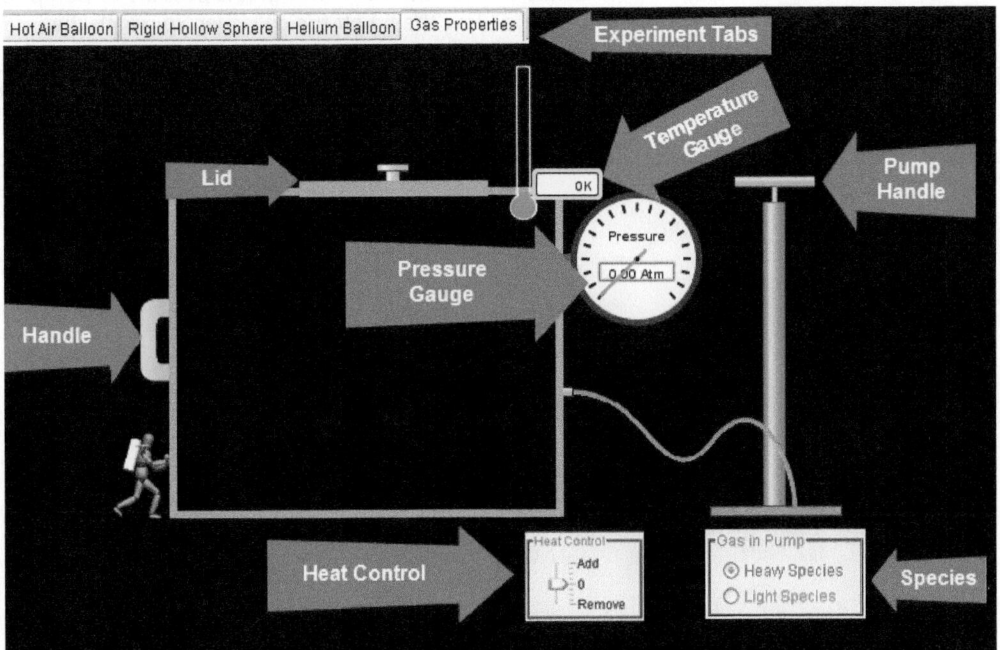

Figure 6-1

Feature	Control
Figure 6-1	
Experiment Tabs	This simulation has four different experiments that you can perform. For this lab, you will use the *Helium Balloon* and *Gas Properties* tabs.
Handle	Click and drag the handle to the left and right to change the width of the chamber.
Lid	Remove the lid on the chamber by clicking and dragging it to the left or right. Note: If you apply too much pressure in the simulation and the lid blows off, you must reset the simulation to place the lid back on the chamber.
Pressure Gauge	You can monitor the amount of pressure inside of the chamber by looking at the pressure gauge.
Temperature Gauge	You can monitor the temperature inside the chamber by looking at the temperature gauge.
Heat Control	Increase the temperature inside the chamber by moving the slider bar on the Heat Control panel up toward *Add*. Decrease the temperature inside the chamber by moving the slider bar on the Heat Control panel down toward *Remove*.
Pump Handle	To add pressure to the chamber, click and drag the pump handle upward then downward. It is possible to pump too hard and blow the lid off the chamber, so watch the pressure gauge as you apply pressure.
Species	The Species panel allows you to pick the type of gas in the pump as *Heavy Species* or *Light* Species. For this lab, select *Heavy Species*.

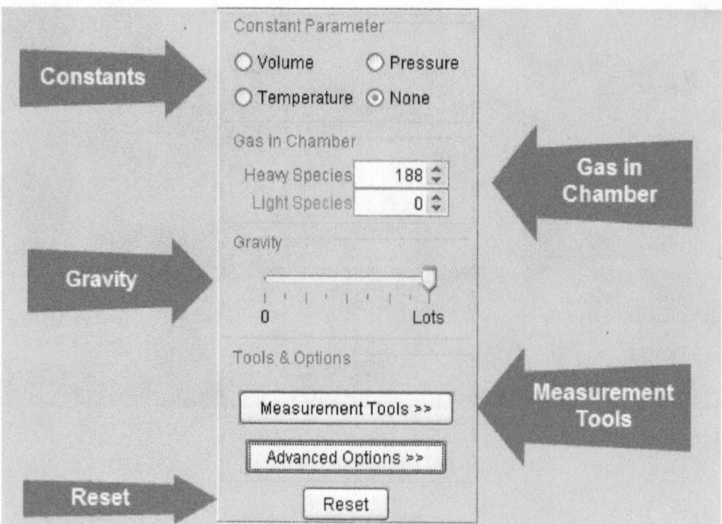

Figure 6-2

Feature	Control
Constants	The *Constants* panel (Figure 6-2) allows you to make volume, pressure, or temperature a constant parameter for your experiments. For this lab, select *None*.
Gas in Chamber	The *Gas in Chamber* panel shown in Figure 6-2 can be adjusted manually. For this experiment, you will not need to adjust this setting because the pump will do this automatically for you.
Gravity	Set the gravity for the experiment by clicking and dragging the slider bar.
Measurement Tools	Click the *Measurement Tools* button, pictured in Figure 6-2, to display all the available measurement tools for the simulation as shown in Figure 6-3. You will use the *Layer Tool* and *Ruler* for this experiment. Figure 6-4 shows how the layer tool appears in the simulation. A box appears that displays *pressure* (P, given in atmospheres) and *height*. Click and drag the box up and down and the numbers will change according to what pressure is in the box at that particular height. Click and drag the ruler to where you want it positioned. The units of the ruler are nm.
	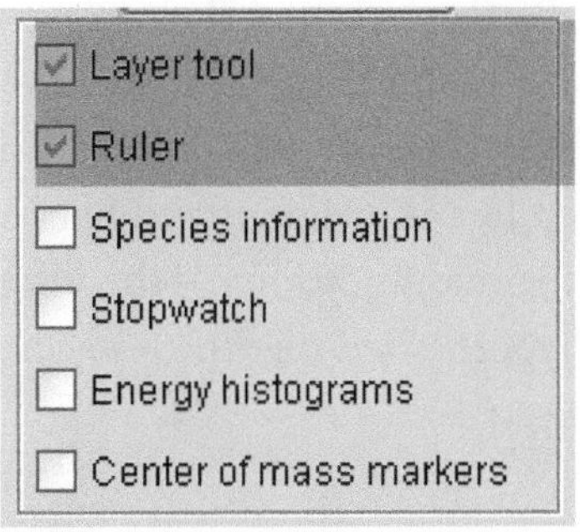 Layer tool Ruler Species information Stopwatch Energy histograms Center of mass markers **Figure 6-3** 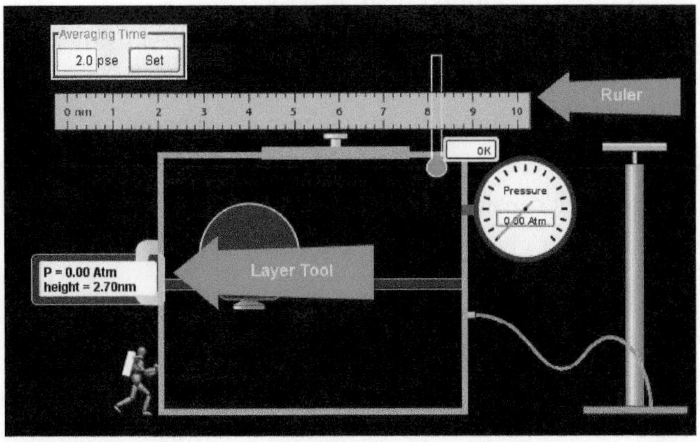 Averaging Time 2.0 pse Set Ruler OK Pressure 0.00 Atm P = 0.00 Atm height = 2.70nm Layer Tool **Figure 6-4**

Continues

Feature	Control
Helium in Balloon	In addition to the options displayed in Figure 6-2, when you click on the *Helium Balloon* experiment, you will see the *Helium in Balloon* panel. You can add atoms inside of the balloon either by typing the number of desired atoms in directly or by clicking the up arrow as shown in Figure 6-5. **Figure 6-5**
Reset	Pushing the *Reset* button only resets the simulation. It does not restore any of the settings.

INTRODUCTION

Since the time of Archimedes, scientists have struggled to properly describe the dynamics of floating objects. Everyone has seen objects floating in water; solids like wood or liquids like oil. You have also seen hot air balloons and blimps float through the air. All of these things can be described using the buoyancy force—the force that pushes upward on the object.

Archimedes hypothesized that the buoyancy force is equal to the weight of the material displaced by the object:

$$F_b = mg = V\rho g$$

Here V is the volume of the material displaced, ρ is the density of the displaced material, and g is the acceleration due to gravity.

The nature of this force can be conceptualized using atomic theory. Atomic theory concerns the nature of matter and states that matter is composed of discrete units called atoms. An atom is a smallest structural unit of a chemical element. Atoms may combine to form a molecule. When a molecule is formed, the atoms' inner electron shells remain almost unchanged, while the outer shell consists of collectivized (shared) electrons. Collisions of these atoms or molecules with the object give rise to the buoyancy force.

The physical systems we can see consist of an enormous number of atoms or molecules that make up so-called macroscopic bodies. Under normal conditions, a macroscopic body contains about 10^{25} to 10^{28} atoms/m^3. To study macroscopic bodies, like volumes of gases, physicists apply the principles of statistics. This gives rise to statistical physics, and in particular, to kinetic theory of gases and thermodynamics. According to these theories, physical variables like pressure, temperature, entropy, and others are macroscopic quantities obtained as statistical averages of the corresponding microscopic quantities (the forces, velocities, and kinetic energies of each particular atom or molecule).

As a good approximation to the behavior of many real gases (at low densities), the concept of a hypothetical ideal gas was suggested. The state of an ideal gas is determined by three parameters: pressure, volume, and temperature (p, V, T). The equation of state of an ideal gas was first suggested by Émile Clapeyron in 1834 as a combination of Boyle's law and Charles's law. The **Ideal Gas Law** takes the form:

$$p \cdot V = k_B \cdot N \cdot T$$

where $k_B = 1.38 \cdot 10^{-23} \frac{J}{K}$ (the Boltzmann constant), N is the number of molecules in volume V in cubic meters, p is the pressure measured in pascals, and T is the absolute temperature measured in Kelvin.

To solve some practical problems, we can use the Ideal Gas Law in the form:

$$\frac{p \cdot V}{T} = constant$$

In particular, given an ideal gas in two different states (p_1, V_1, T_1) and (p_2, V_2, T_2), we have:

$$\frac{p_1 \cdot V_1}{T_1} = \frac{p_2 \cdot V_2}{T_2}$$

We can solve the last equation for any unknown variable.

In this lab, you will explore the macroscopic quantities of pressure, volume, and temperature and their effect on the motion of atoms. You will test the idea of the buoyancy force and describe it in terms of atomic theory.

PROCEDURES

Part 1

1. Apply the following settings to the Gas Properties simulation:

    i. Maximize the screen.
    ii. *Gravity* should be set to **0**.
    iii. Select **Gas Properties** on the *Experiment Tabs.*
    iv. Select **Heavy Species** for the *Gas in Pump* panel.
    v. Move the pump handle up and down twice.
    vi. Increase *Gravity* to **lots**.
    vii. Select the **Layer Tool** from the *Measurement Tools* Panel.

    If you have correctly applied the settings, your screen will look similar to Figure 6-6.

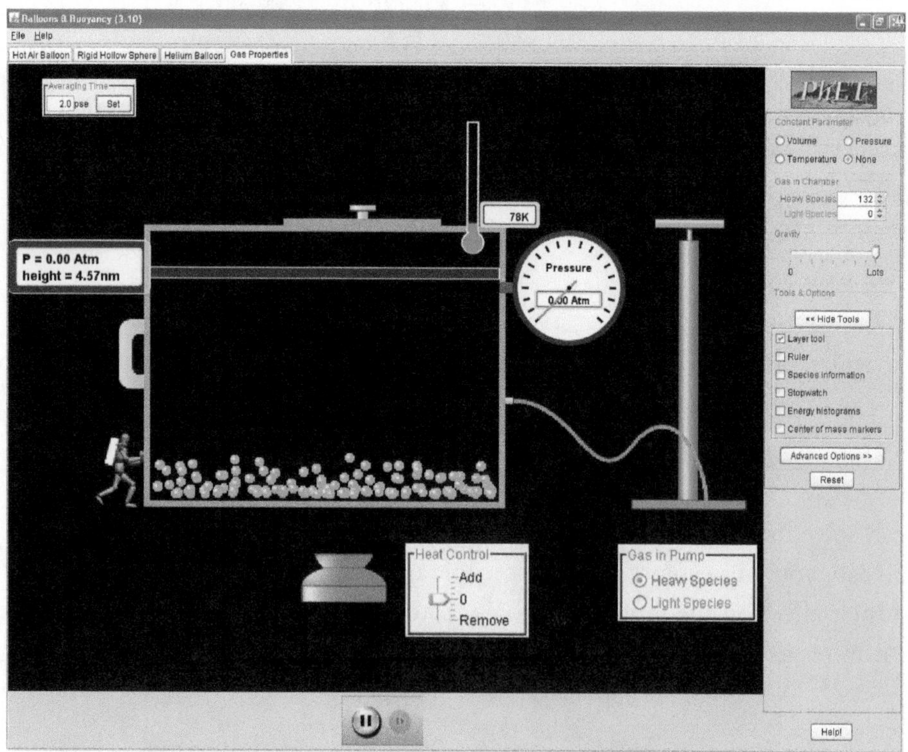

Figure 6-6

2. Using the *Layer tool*, determine where in the chamber the pressure is:

   a. The highest: ________________
   b. The lowest: ________________

3. Why is the pressure different in different areas of the chamber?
4. Decrease *Gravity* to **0** and reduce the chamber to half its original size. Your screen should look similar to Figure 6-7.

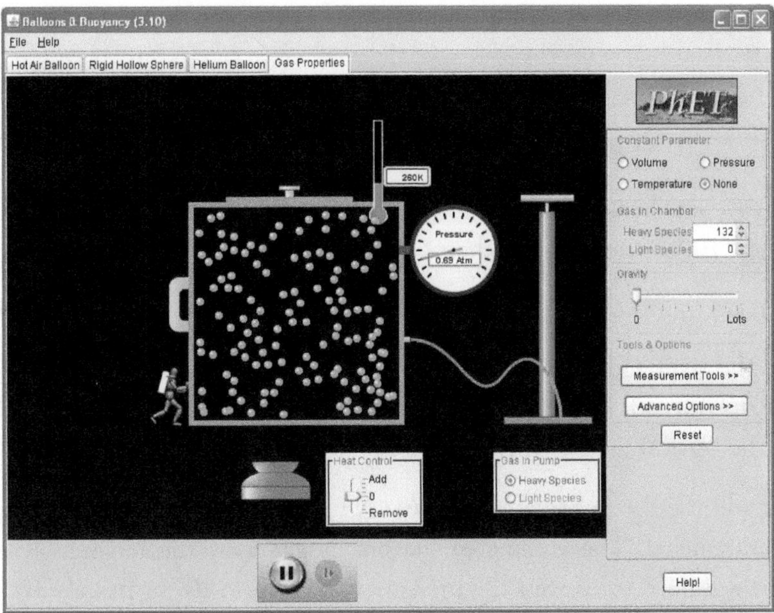

Figure 6-7

5. Write your responses to the following:

   a. What happens to the temperature and pressure in the box?

b. Describe the motion of the atoms.

c. How is pressure related to the motion of the atoms?

6. Click the Reset button. Reapply all the settings as described in Step 1 *except*

   a. Leave gravity set to zero.
   b. Add 100 atoms into the chamber.

7. Turn on the *Ruler* and the *Layer Tool.* Move the *Layer Tool* to the top of the chamber.

   Use the layer tool and the ruler to measure the two dimensions visible on the screen. Use the ruler for the horizontal measurement of the box (side to side). Use the layer tool for the vertical measurement of the box (top to bottom).

   You will use the formula $p \cdot V = k_B \cdot N \cdot T$ to find the depth of the box (front to back measurement). The volume of the box is given by the formula $V = W \times H \times D$. (You will need to convert the pressure from atm to Pa, or pascals, by multiplying atms by 1×10^5.) See Figure 6-8.

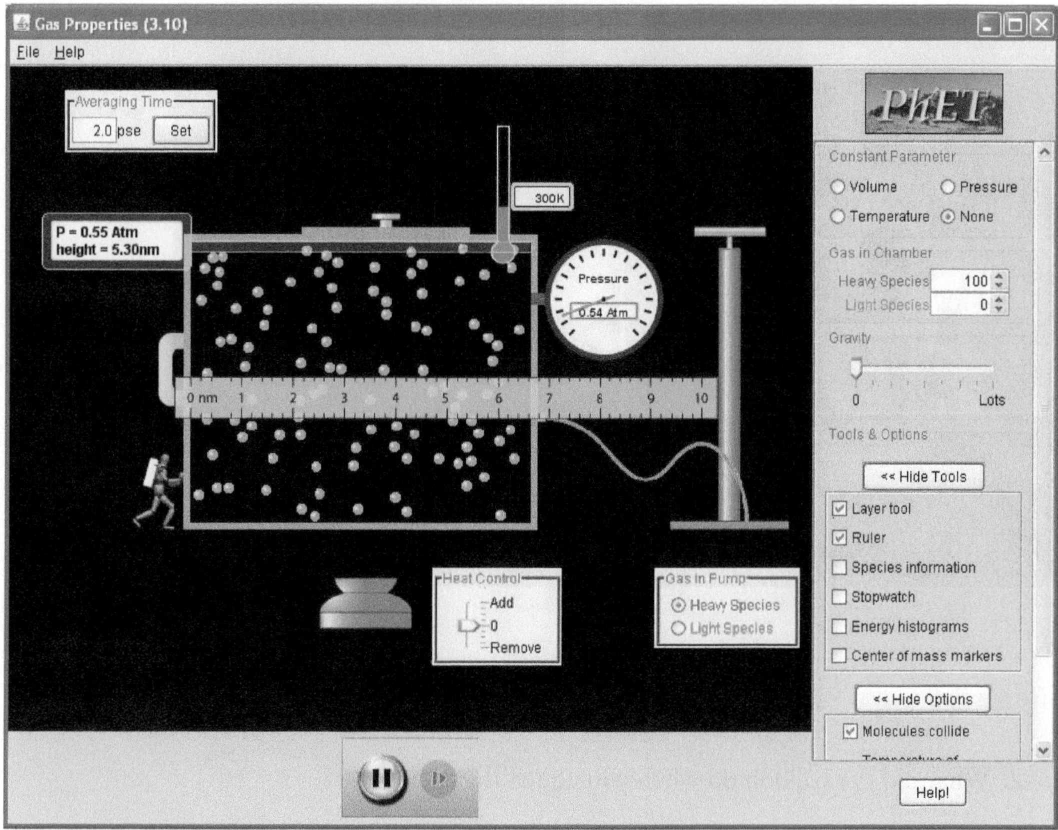

Figure 6-8

Part 2

1. Apply the following settings to the simulation:

   a. On the *Experiment Tab*, select **Helium Balloon.**
   b. Set *Gravity* **exactly between 0 and Lots.**
   c. Select **Heavy Species** for the *Gas in Chamber* panel.
   d. Hide *Measurement Tools.*
   e. Set the *Helium in Balloon* panel to **25** atoms.

   If you have correctly applied the settings, your screen will look similar to Figure 6-9 and begin to change.

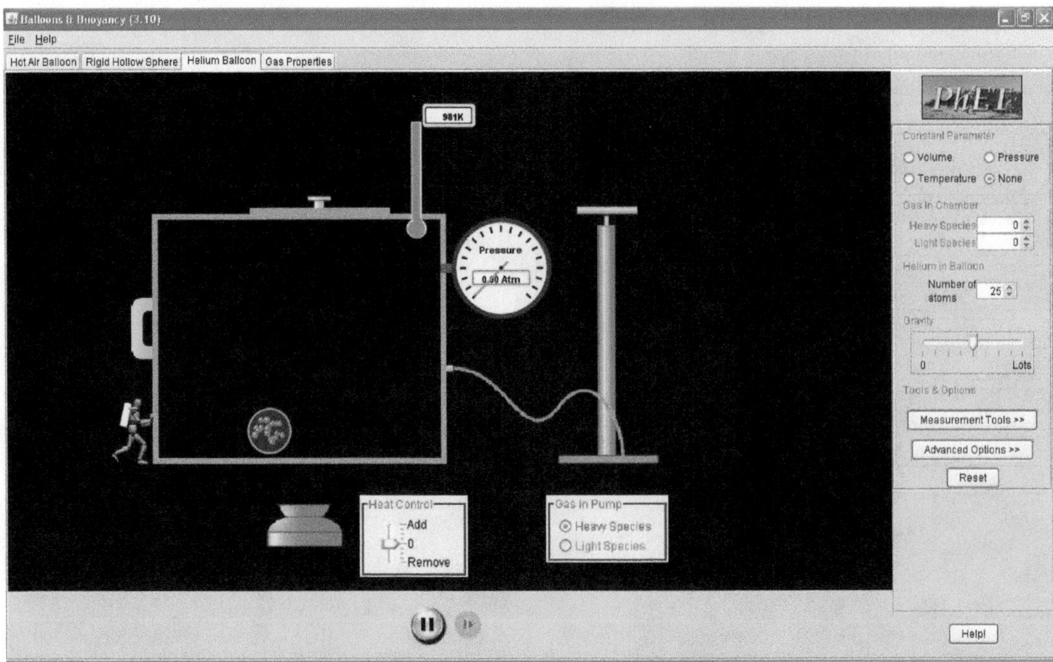

Figure 6-9

2. What did the balloon do when you added the 25 atoms?

3. Type **100** into the *Heavy Species* box located on the Gas in Chamber panel.

4. What happened to the balloon when you added gas into the chamber?

5. Based on your observations of the experiment, describe the buoyancy of the balloon.

6. Move the slider bar upward on the *Heat Control* panel until the temperature is over 1000°K. Describe the pressure in both the box and balloon. Describe the motion of the atoms.

QUESTIONS

1. Describe pressure in terms of the motion of atoms.

2. List two ways to manipulate a reduction of temperature within the chamber.

3. Describe the concept of buoyancy in terms of the motion of atoms as you observed in this experiment.

7

TEMPERATURE AND HEAT

PURPOSE

The purpose of this lab is to investigate phases of matter, temperature, and heat energy.

SIMULATIONS

States of Matter

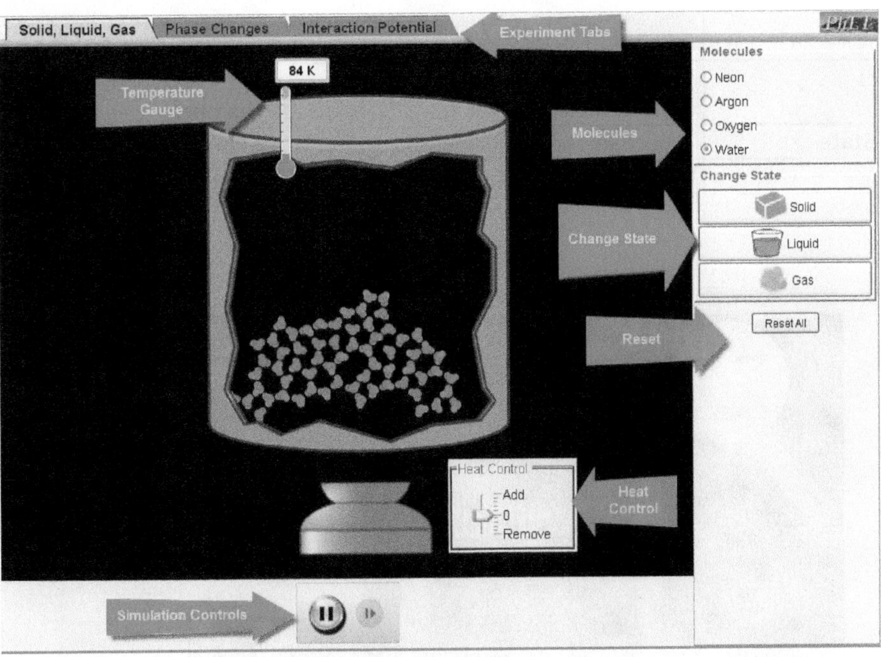

Figure 7-1: Solid, Liquid, and Gas Tab

Feature	Control
Figure 7-1: Solid, Liquid, and Gas Tab	
Experiment Tabs	This simulation lets you perform three different experiments. For Part 1 of this lab, you will use the *Solid, Liquid, and Gas* tab.
Temperature Gauge	You can monitor the temperature inside the chamber by looking at the temperature gauge.
Heat Control	Increase the temperature inside the chamber by moving the slider bar on the *Heat Control* panel up toward *Add*. Decrease the temperature by moving the slider bar down toward *Remove*.
Simulation Controls	Pause the simulation by clicking the button shown in Figure 7-2. After pausing the simulation, you can continue playing the simulation at full speed by pressing button A shown in Figure 7-3. To move through the simulation in steps, press button B. A B Figure 7-2 Figure 7-3
Molecules	Use the *Molecules* panel to choose neon, argon, oxygen, or water as the type of molecule that appears inside the chamber.
Change State	Select among solid, liquid, or gas on the *Change State* panel.
Reset	Click the *Reset All* button to return the simulation to its default values.

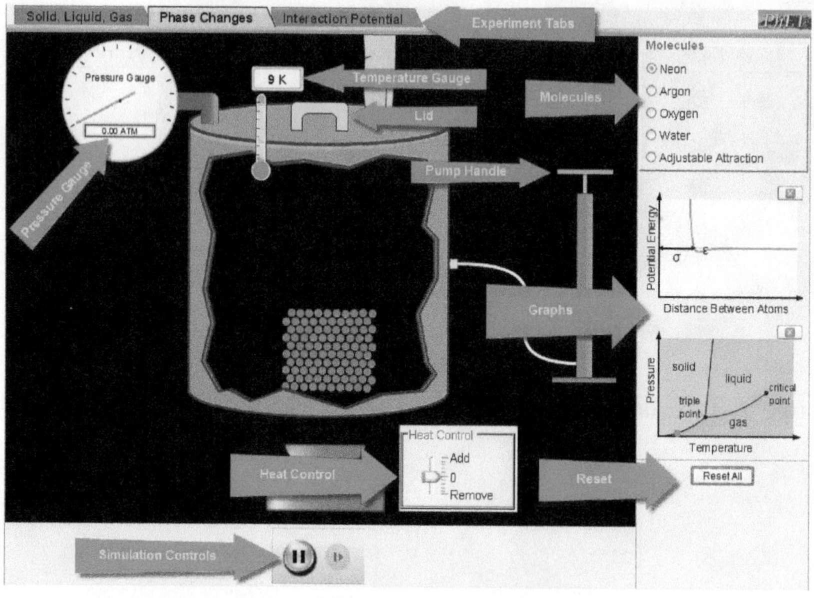

Figure 7-4: Phase Changes Tab

Feature	**Control**
	Figure 7-4: Phase Changes Tab
Experiment Tabs	This simulation lets you perform three different experiments. For Part 2 of this lab, you will use the *Phase Changes* tab.
Temperature Gauge	You can monitor the temperature inside the chamber by looking at the temperature gauge.
Pressure Gauge	You can monitor the amount of pressure inside of the container by looking at the pressure gauge. It is possible to apply so much pressure that the lid blows off the container. If this happens, reset the simulation to replace the lid back onto the chamber.
Lid	Click on the lid and drag downward to push the lid on the chamber down. You may pull the lid back up by clicking and dragging the lid upward.
Heat Control	Increase the temperature inside the chamber by moving the slider bar on the *Heat Control* panel up toward *Add*. Decrease the temperature by moving the slider bar down toward *Remove*.
Simulation Controls	Pause the simulation by clicking the button shown in Figure 7-2. After pausing the simulation, you can continue playing the simulation at full speed by pressing button A shown in Figure 7-3. To move through the simulation in steps, press button B. Figure 7-2 A B Figure 7-3
Molecules	Use the *Molecules* panel to choose neon, argon, oxygen, water, or adjustable attraction for the type of molecule that appears inside the chamber.
Reset	Click the Reset *All* button to return the simulation to its default values.
Graphs	The graph panel contains two graphs: Potential Energy and Pressure. For this lab, close the Potential Energy graph by clicking on the located in the upper right-hand corner of the graph.
Pump Handle	To add molecules to the container, click and drag the pump handle upward then downward.

INTRODUCTION

Heat is a form of energy associated with the motion of atoms and molecules. Heat energy can be transferred from one body or system to another body or a system through thermal contact or radiation. The energy flows from the warmer body to the cooler body. You can see this happen by holding an ice cube in your hand—your heat is transferred to the solid water. This also demonstrates that heat energy can be directly used to increase the internal energy of matter.

As the internal energy of the matter increases, so does the kinetic energy of its atoms and molecules. This can be seen in the motion of the atoms and molecules. The concept is referred to as kinetic theory.

Temperature, volume, and pressure are all related. Changing one affects the other two and all of them affect the phase of the matter involved. The three quantities—pressure, volume, and temperature—can be used to define any state of matter.

In this lab, you will investigate the effect of temperature and pressure on the different phases of matter. You will also use kinetic theory to help describe the different phases and phase transitions.

PROCEDURES

Part 1

1. Apply the following settings to the simulation:

   a. Maximize the screen.
   b. Select the *Solid, Liquid, Gas* tab.
   c. Select **Water** on the *Molecules* panel.
   d. Leave the Heat Control set at 0.

   If you have correctly applied the settings, your screen will look similar to Figure 7-5.
2. Click the blue Pause button. Select **Solid** on the *Change State* panel.

   a. Describe the shape the molecules take and the interactions that occur the instant you select solid state.

3. Click the Play button (Button A in Figure 7-3).

   a. Watch the molecules in the container for 15–30 seconds. What happens over time as you watch the solid?

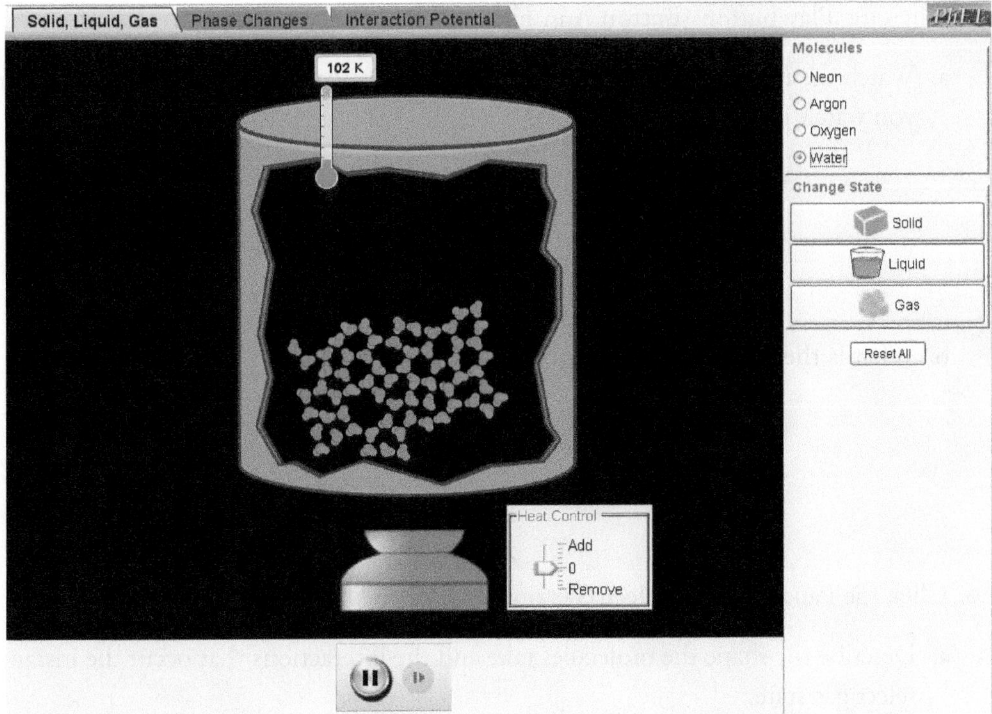

Figure 7-5

b. What is the current temperature?

4. Click the Pause button. Select **Liquid** on the *Change State* panel. Keep **Water** selected on the *Molecules* panel.

   a. Describe the shape the molecules take and the interactions that occur the instant you select liquid state.

5. Click the Play button (Button A in Figure 7-3).

   a. Watch the molecules in the container for 15–30 seconds. What happens over time as you watch the liquid?

   b. What is the current temperature?

6. Click the Pause button. Select **Gas** on the *Change State* panel.

   a. Describe the shape the molecules take and the interactions that occur the instant you select gas state.

7. Click the Play button (Button A in Figure 7-3).

   a. Watch the molecules in the container for 15–30 seconds. What happens over time as you watch the gas?

   b. What is the current temperature?

8. Using the Heat Control slider, remove heat energy from the container. Lower the temperature to 250K. Describe the current phase of the water.

9. Remove more heat energy from the container. Lower the temperature to less than 90K. Describe the current phase of the water.

Part 2

1. Apply the following settings to the simulation:

   a. Maximize the screen.
   b. Select the *Phase Changes* tab.
   c. Select **Neon** on the *Molecules* panel. Neon is a monatomic gas; it exists as single atoms rather than molecules.
   d. On the *Graph* panel, close the Potential Energy graph.
   e. Using the pump handle, apply four pumps of gas.

   If you have correctly applied the settings, your screen will look similar to Figure 7-6.

2. Describe the motion of the new atoms as they enter the container. What do they do after they are inside?

3. Push the lid of the container down so that it increases the pressure inside of the container. Keep pushing the lid down until the Pressure vs. Temperature chart shows the red dot in the liquid region. How would you characterize the matter now?

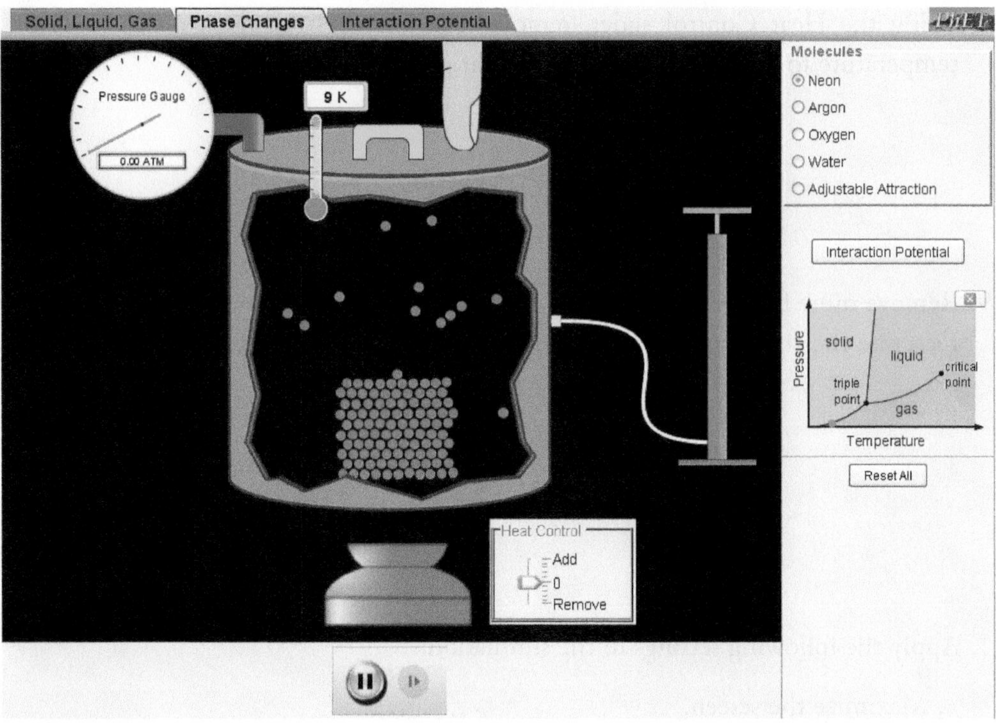

Figure 7-6

4. Return the lid to the original position and raise the temperature to 100K. Did the temperature rise quickly? Why or why not?

5. Slowly increase the pressure by pushing the lid down. What happens to the temperature?

QUESTIONS

1. In what phase are the atoms not moving?

2. Can the molecules in the container be in more than one phase at a time?

3. Describe a way to raise the temperature of matter without using heat energy.

4. What happens to the motion of the atoms as you increase the heat energy?

8

ELECTRICITY

PURPOSE

The purpose of this lab is to investigate electric fields and potentials.

SIMULATIONS

Charges and Fields

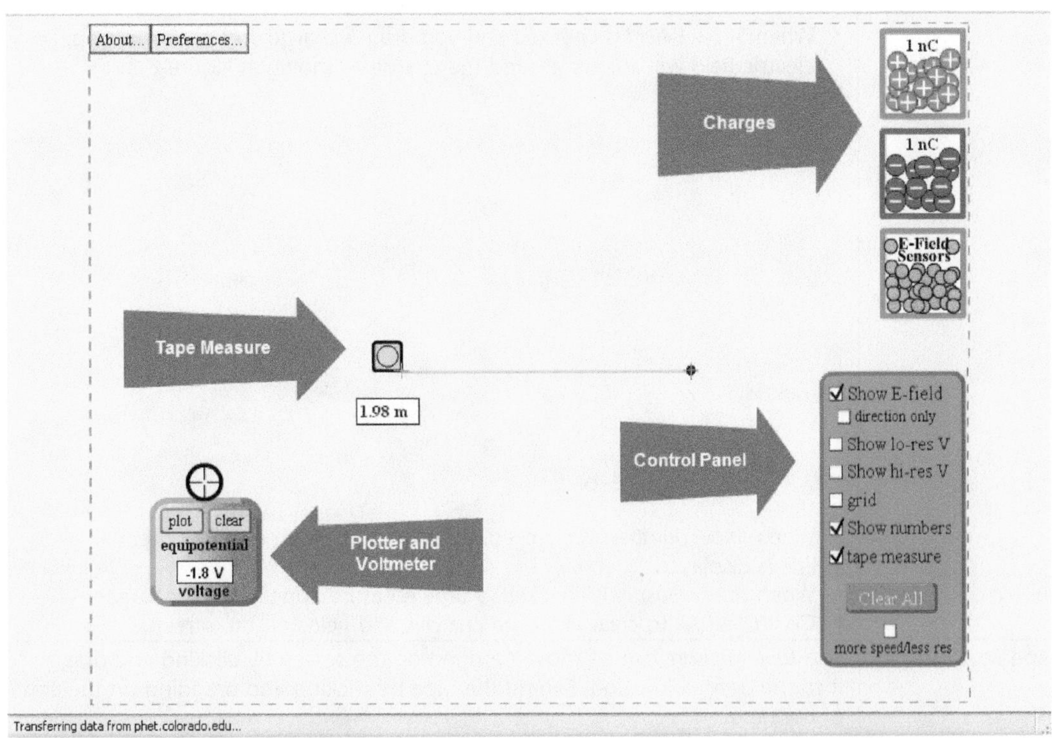

Figure 8-1

Feature	Control
	Figure 8-1
Charges	You can drag positive and negative charges out of their respective boxes and onto the map (work area inside the dotted-line box). Click and drag a circle out of the box and place it on the map as shown in Figure 8-2. 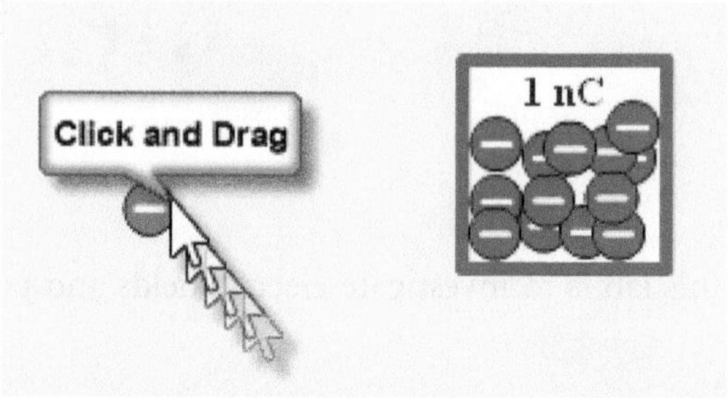 Figure 8-2
Control Panel	For this lab, you will use the following features on the control panel: *Show E-field, Show numbers, tape measure, Clear All* • When *Show E-field* is checked and you drag a charge and onto the map, an electric field will appear around the charge as shown in Figure 8-3. 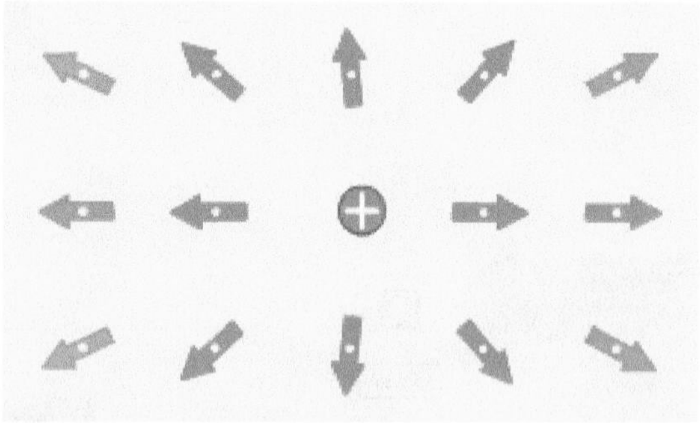 Figure 8-3 • When *Show numbers* is checked, the voltage of each electric potential field line is displayed. • When *tape measure* is checked, a tape measure appears on the screen. • Click Clear All to clear all of the charges and fields on the screen.
Tape Measure	The *tape measure* can be moved around on the screen by clicking and dragging it to the desired location. Extend the tape by clicking and dragging on the end of the tape.

Feature	Control
Plotter and Voltmeter	The *Plotter and Voltmeter* panel serves two functions. • When you click the *plot* button, an electric potential field is plotted around a charge. Click and drag the *Plotter and Voltmeter* where you want a field drawn. Then click plot. See Figure 8-4. Click *clear* to delete all of the fields that have been drawn. 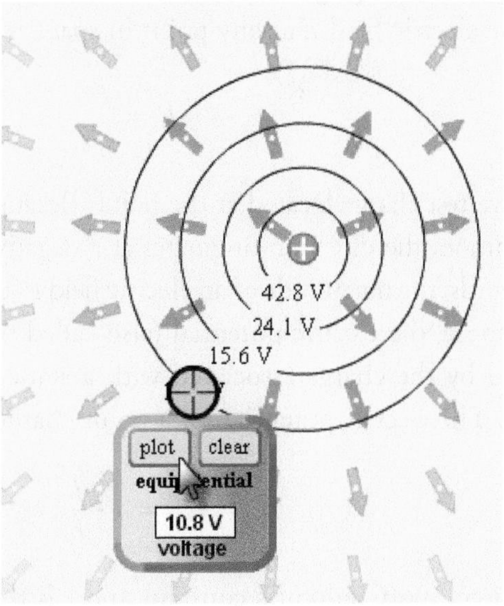 Figure 8-4 • The voltmeter shows the electric potential based on its current position when a charge is present.

INTRODUCTION

Electricity is present everywhere you look. It is used to power devices and governs the properties of all matter. Understanding electric forces, electric fields, and potentials are key concepts to understanding electricity.

The most basic area to start with is electrostatics. Electrostatics is the study of non-moving charges.

Electric charges interact with each other because of attractive or repulsive electric forces. The magnitude of an electric force between two electric point charges in free space is defined by Coulomb's Law:

$$F = k \cdot \frac{q_1 \cdot q_2}{r^2}$$

where q_1 and q_2 are the charges measured in Coulombs, $k = 8.988 \times 10^9 \frac{N \cdot m^2}{C^2}$ (also called Coulomb's constant of proportionality), and r is the distance measured in meters between charges. An electric force is a vector quantity that acts along a straight line from one charge to the other.

The electric field is a property of space surrounding electric charges. Electric charges, whether stationary or moving, generate an electric vector field in their vicinity. The strength (magnitude) of the electric field E at any point in space is defined by the formula:

$$E = \frac{F}{q}$$

where q is a positive test charge located at the point. Because the electric field is a vector, it has a direction. By definition, the direction originates at a negative charge and terminates at a positive change. In other words, the magnitude of an electric field is just the electric force per unit of charge.

At a point in space, the electric potential (also called the "electrostatic potential") is potential energy divided by the charge associated with a static electric field. It is a scalar quantity, measured in volts. The electric potential (of a point charge only) in free space is defined as:

$$V = k \cdot \frac{q}{r}$$

where q is the charge, k is Coulomb's constant and r is the distance between the charge and a point at which the potential is measured.

The electric force and potential can be used to describe the interactions of charges with one another.

In this lab, you will work with static (unmoving) charges and compare calculated electric potentials with measured electric potentials. You will also describe how the electric field is defined for different charge configurations.

PROCEDURES

Part 1: One Charge

1. Apply the following settings to the simulation:

   a. Maximize the screen.
   b. Check **Show E-field** on the *Control Panel.*
   c. Check **Show numbers** on the *Control Panel.*
   d. Check **tape measure** on the *Control Panel.*

   If you have correctly applied the settings, your screen will look similar to Figure 8-1.
2. Drag a negative $1nC$ charge onto the map as shown in Figure 8-5.

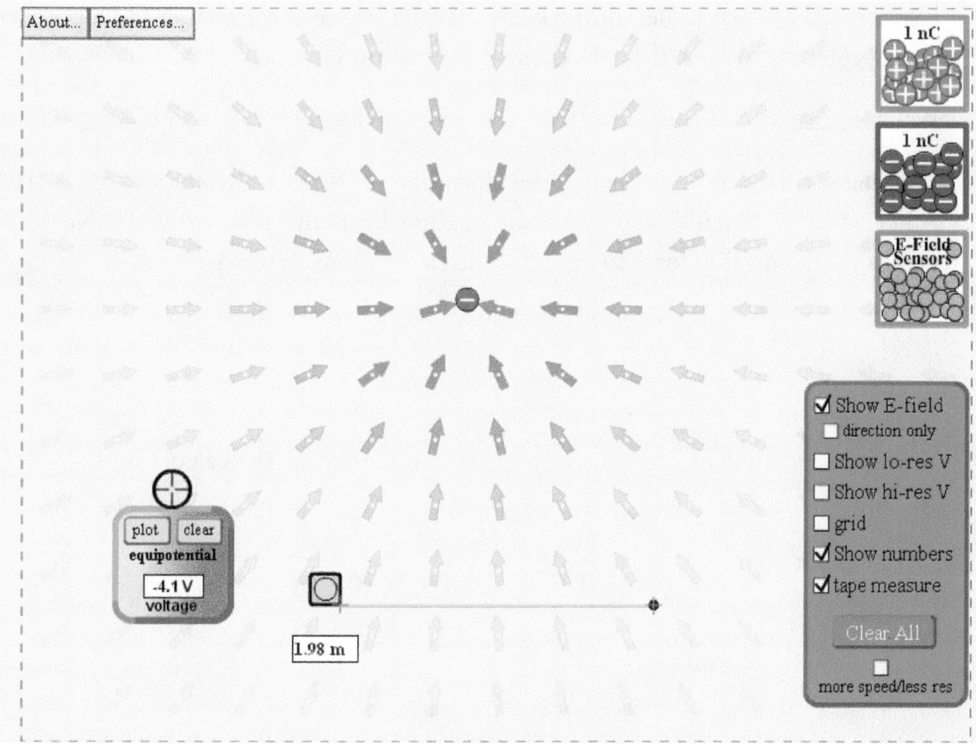

Figure 8-5

3. Position the *Plotter and Voltmeter* close to your charge and click *plot* to draw a potential line around the charge. Do this three more times, each time moving a little further away from the charge. You should have four potential lines (circles) drawn around the charge similar to Figure 8-4.
4. Draw the electric field and electric potential lines in the space below. Make sure you include in your details the strength of the electric field. The strength is indicated by how clear and focused the arrows are in the simulation—lighter, fuzzier arrows signify lower strength; sharper, darker arrows signify higher strength.

5. Use the *tape measure* to determine r, the distance between the charge and a point on any one of the four potential lines (circles) you just drew.

   r = ________ m

6. Calculate the potential using the formula $V = k \cdot \frac{q}{r}$ where $k = 9 \times 10^9$, $q = -1nC = -1 \times 10^{-9}$ and r is your reading from the tape measure. Note: We are usinga rounded value for k to simplify the calculations. Show your work.

Here is an example of how to apply the measurements to the calculations.

Given:

$$q = -1nC = -1.00 \times 10^{-9}C$$

$$r = 0.269\ m$$

$$k = 9.00 \times 10^9 \frac{N \cdot m^2}{C^2}$$

$$V = -32.9V$$

Note: For this lab, V represents the actual potential and $\hat{V}$ represents the calculated potential. The actual potential will not be used until Step 6.

Find the voltage in a point located at the given distance from the charge and compare it to the given voltage.

Solution:

Calculate the potential using the formula $\hat{V} = k \cdot \frac{q}{r}$:

$$\hat{V} = (9.00 \times 10^9 \frac{N \cdot m^2}{C^2}) \cdot \frac{(-1.00 \times 10^{-9}C)}{0.269m} = -33.5 \frac{N}{C} = -33.5V$$

Calculated potential (show your work):

7. How does your calculated potential compare to the actual potential?

   Here is an example based on the example in Step 5.

Since $\frac{\hat{V}-V}{V}=\frac{-33.5V-(-32.9V)}{-32.9V}=0.02$, the relative error of measurements is approximately 2%.

Actual potential: ______________ V
Comparison (show your work):

8. Click the *Clear all* button on the Control Panel. This time, drag a positive $1nC$ charge onto the map.
9. Use the Plotter and Voltmeter to draw four potential lines around the charge as you did in Step 3.
10. Draw the electric field and electric potential lines in the space below. Make sure you include in your details the strength of the electric field. The strength is indicated by how clear and focused the arrows are in the simulation—lighter, fuzzier arrows signify lower strength; sharper, darker arrows signify higher strength.

11. Use the *tape measure* to determine r, the distance between the charge and any one of the four potential lines (circles) you just drew.

r = __________ m

12. Calculate the potential using the formula $V = k \cdot \frac{q}{r}$, where $k = 9.00 \times 10^9 \frac{N \cdot m^2}{C^2}$, $q = +1nC = +1.00 \times 10^{-9}C$ and r is your reading from the tape measure.

Note: We are using a rounded value for k to simplify the calculations. Show your work.

Here is an example of measurements and calculations.

For the charge given:

$$q = +1nC = +1.00 \times 10^{-9}C$$
$$r = 0.269m$$
$$k = 9.00 \times 10^9 \frac{N \cdot m^2}{C^2}$$
$$V = 32.9\ V$$

Note: For this lab, V represents the actual potential and $\hat{V}$ represents the calculated potential. The actual potential will not be used until Step 13.

Find the voltage in a point located at the given distance from the charge and compare it to the given voltage.

Solution:

Use the formula $\hat{V} = k \cdot \frac{q}{r}$ to calculate the following:

$$\hat{V} = (9.00 \times 10^9 \frac{N \cdot m^2}{C^2}) \cdot \frac{(1.00 \times 10^{-9}C)}{0.269\ m} = 33.5 \frac{N}{C} = 33.5V$$

Calculated potential (show your work):

13. How does the calculated potential compare to the actual potential as shown on the potential line?

    Actual potential: _________ V

    Comparison (show your work):

Part 2: Two Charges

1. Click the *Clear all* button located on the Control Panel. Drag a positive and negative charge onto the map as shown in Figure 8-6.

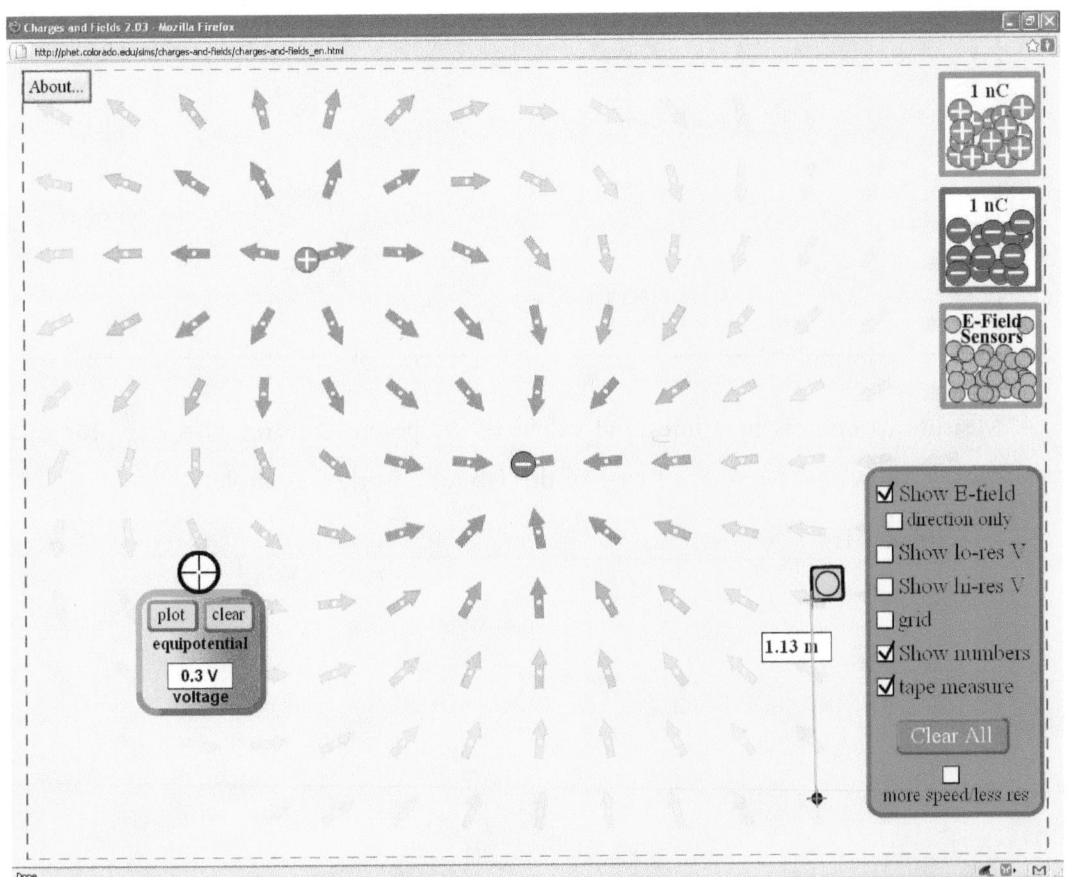

Figure 8-6

2. Use the *Plotter and Voltmeter* to draw four potential lines around each charge.

3. Draw the electric field and electric potential lines in the space below. Make sure you include in your details the strength of the electric field. The strength is indicated by how clear and focused the arrows are in the simulation—lighter, fuzzier arrows signify lower strength; sharper, darker arrows signify higher strength.

4. Measure to one of these lines and calculate the potential using $V = k \cdot \frac{q}{r}$, for each charge. Show your work. See Part 1 of this lab for a worked example.

Potential 1:

Potential 2:

5. Add the two values and compare the result to the actual potential as shown on the potential line.

   Sum of Potential 1 and 2: ___________ V

QUESTIONS

1. How does the strength of the electric fields change as you move closer and further away from the charges?

2. Describe the relationship of the field lines and the potential lines where they cross.

3. Compare the potential lines when charges are initially close together versus when they are initially far apart.

9

WAVES

PURPOSE

The purpose of this lab is to investigate waves and properties of waves.

SIMULATIONS

Wave on a String

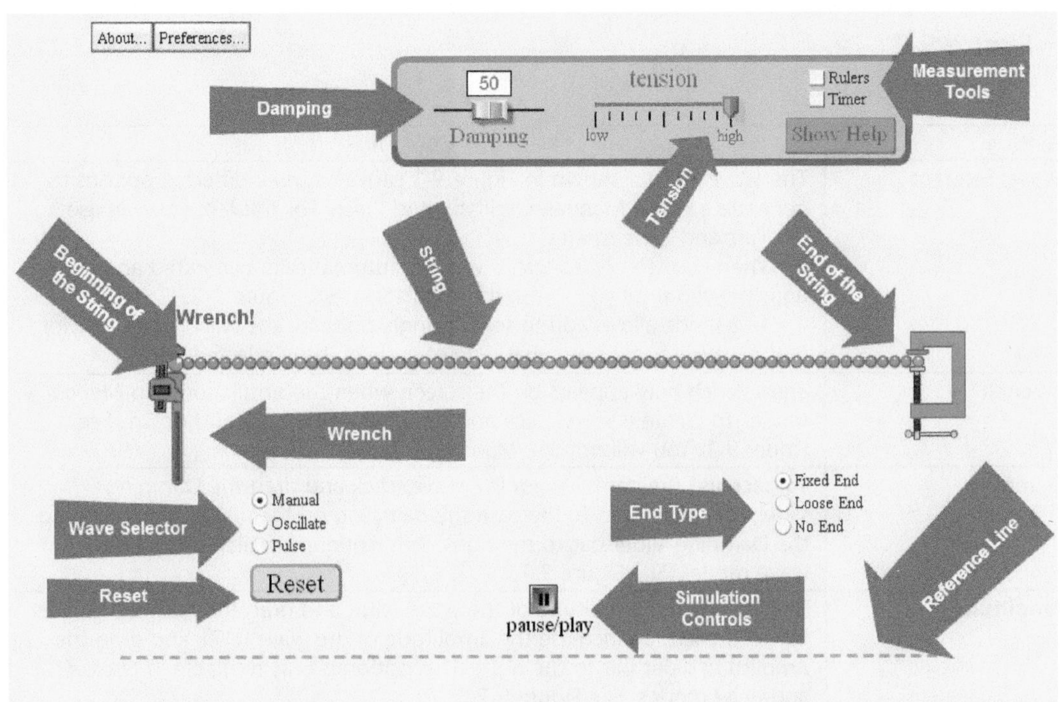

Figure 9-1

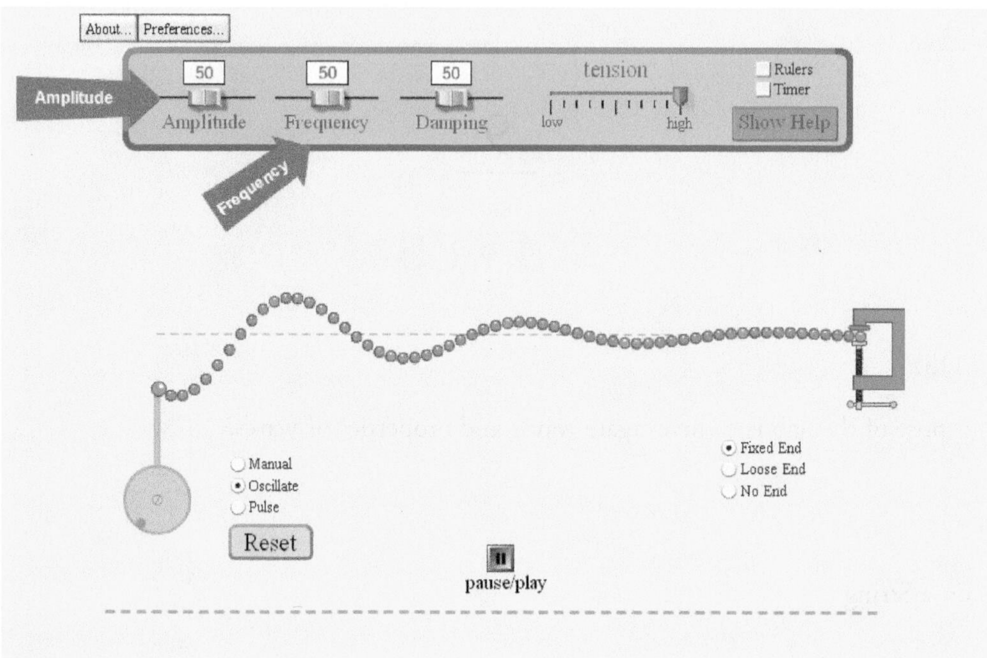

Figure 9-2

Feature	Control
Wave Selector	The *Wave Selector* shown in Figure 9-1 provides three different options to generate a wave: Manual, Oscillate, and Pulse. For this lab, you will use *Oscillate* and *Pulse* modes. When you select *Oscillate*, a wave is automatically generated and continuously cycles until you pause the simulation. See Figure 9-2. *Pulse* mode allows you to send a single pulse for the wave. The behavior of the wave depends on what type of end you have selected.
Wrench	The wrench only appears on the screen when the simulation is in *Manual* mode. To create a wave, click and drag the wrench up and down. See Figure 9-1. You will not use *Manual* mode in this lab.
Damping	To decrease the damping on the wave, click and drag the Damping slider bar to the left. To increase the damping on the wave, click and drag the Damping slider bar to the right. This option is available in all three wave modes. See Figure 9-1.
Amplitude	To decrease the amplitude of the wave, click and drag the Amplitude slider bar to the left. To increase the amplitude of the wave, click and drag the Amplitude slider bar to the right. This option is only available in *Oscillate* and *Pulse* modes. See Figure 9-2.

Feature	Control
Frequency	To decrease the frequency of the wave, click and drag the Frequency slider bar to the left. To increase the frequency of the wave, click and drag the Frequency slider bar to the right. This option is only available in *Oscillate* and *Pulse* modes. See Figure 9-2.
Measurement Tools	When you check the box labeled *Rulers* shown in Figure 9-1, two rulers appear on the screen as shown in Figure 9-3. You can click and drag them to any location on the screen. For this lab, you will use the upright—vertical—ruler to measure the amplitude of a wave. The sideways—horizontal—ruler will be used to measure the wave length. 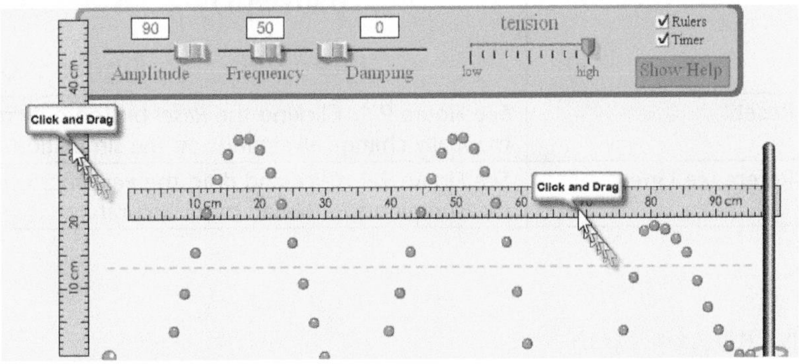 **Figure 9-3** When you check the box labeled *Timer*, a timer appears on the screen as shown in Figure 9-4. You can click and drag the timer to move it to a different location. The timer has a reset button and start/pause button. For this lab, you will use the timer to determine the frequency of a wave.  **Figure 9-4**
End Type	The simulation allows you to pick from three different end types: *Fixed End, Loose End,* and *No End.* See Figure 9-1.

Continues

Feature	Control
Simulation Controls	See Figure 9-1. You can pause by clicking the button pictured in Figure 9-5. After pausing the simulation, you can continue playing the simulation at full speed by pressing button A shown in Figure 9-6. To move through the simulation in steps, press button B. pause/play **Figure 9-5** A B pause/play step **Figure 9-6**
Reset	See Figure 9-1. Clicking the *Reset* button only resets the wave. You must manually change all settings on the simulation.
Reference Line	See Figure 9-1. Click and drag the *Reference Line* to help you perform measurements in the lab more accurately.

INTRODUCTION

Waves are an integral part of our everyday lives. Some examples of where we deal with waves in nature include sound and light, heat radiation, earthquakes, and tsunamis. We use waves in telecommunication (radio and TV), playing a guitar, listening to music, measuring the speed of a car, or medical procedures like X-rays and ultrasounds.

Photo by Roger McLassus, 2006.

A wave is a disturbance that propagates through space and time, usually with the transfer of energy. All waves share some basic features—for example, all waves involve vibration or oscillations. Waves can be characterized as mechanical (in which material moves, such as sound waves, seismic waves, etc.) and non-mechanical (waves that do not involve material, such as electromagnetic waves, gravitational waves, etc.). Mechanical waves require a medium to travel, while non-mechanical waves can travel through a vacuum as well as through a medium. Any kind of wave can carry energy and information from one place of space to another.

In this lab, you will investigate the properties of waves such as amplitude, frequency, and wavelength. You will also investigate how waves interact a medium.

A waveform refers the shape and form of a graph of the varying characteristics vs. time or distance. One of the most important examples of a waveform is a sine wave. Here is a standard sine wave graph:

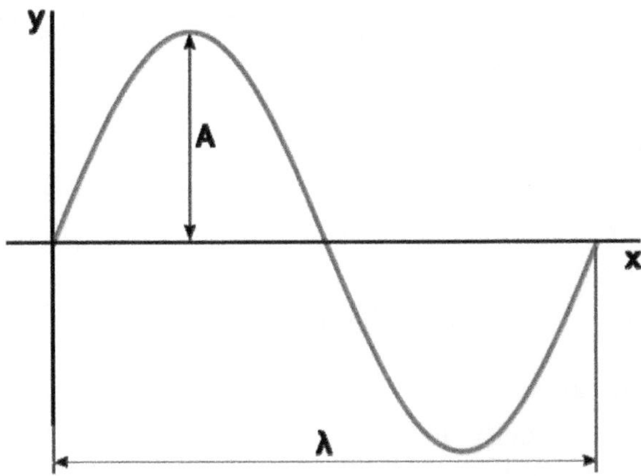

The basic vocabulary describing waves:

- Period T is the time it takes for one complete waveform to pass by a given point in space.
- Frequency f of a wave is the number of complete waveforms passing by a given point in one second.
- Wavelength λ (lambda) is the measured distance for on complete cycle of the wave.
- Wave speed v (or velocity) is a speed with which a fixed point on a waveform travels in space.
- Amplitude A is the highest magnitude of the disturbance of the wave (the maximum displacement of the waveform from its zero level).
- Damping is a measure of friction that slows down motion in oscillations. It affects both the amplitude and frequency of waves. Damping is determined by the value of the damping coefficient.

The characteristics listed above are related by the following equations:

$$f = \frac{1}{T},\ v = \frac{\lambda}{T} = \lambda \cdot f$$

A vibrating string generates a sine wave. A vibrating string, such as a guitar or piano string, also produces a sound whose frequency in most cases is constant. The speed of propagation of a wave in a string (v) is proportional to the square root of the tension of the string (T) and inversely proportional to the square root of the linear mass density (μ) of the string:

$$v = \sqrt{\frac{T}{\mu}}$$

Given the speed of propagation, the lowest (fundamental) frequency of waves produced by the vibrating string with two fixed ends can be calculated using the following formula:

$$f = \frac{v}{2L} = \frac{1}{2L}\sqrt{\frac{T}{\mu}}$$

where L is the length of the string. A wave of the fundamental frequency, called the fundamental harmonics, has the wavelength $\lambda = 2L$.

PROCEDURES

Part 1: Oscillating Waves

1. Apply the following settings to the simulation:

   a. Maximize the screen.
   b. Set *Wave Selector* to **Oscillate.**
   c. Set *End Type* to **No End.**
   d. Set *Amplitude* to **50.**
   e. Set *Frequency* to **50.**
   f. Set *Damping* to **0.**
   g. Set *Tension* to **High.**
   h. Check both boxes on the *Measurement Tools* panel: *Rulers* and *Timer.*

   If you have correctly applied the settings, your screen will look similar to Figure 9-7.

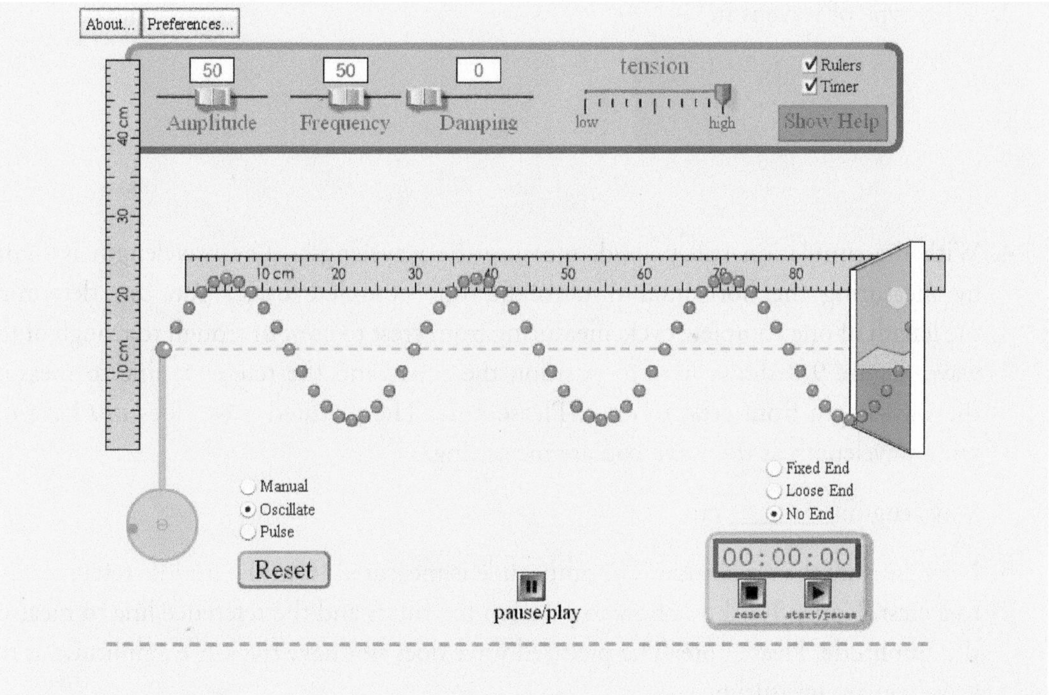

Figure 9-7

2. Click the *pause/play* button to stop the simulation and sketch the wave below.

3. What type of wave is it?

4. With the simulation still paused, measure the wavelength. The wavelength is found by measuring the horizontal distance for one complete cycle. You can determine the length of one complete cycle measuring from crest to crest or trough to trough of the wave. Figure 9-8 shows how to position the rulers and the reference line to measure the wavelength from crest to crest. Please note: The pictured wave does ***not*** have the same wavelength as the wave you are measuring.

   Wavelength: _______ cm

5. Now measure the amplitude. The amplitude is measured from the middle reference line to a crest. Figure 9-8 shows how to position the rulers and the reference line to measure the amplitude. Please note: The pictured wave does ***not*** have the same amplitude as the wave you are measuring.

   Amplitude: _______ cm

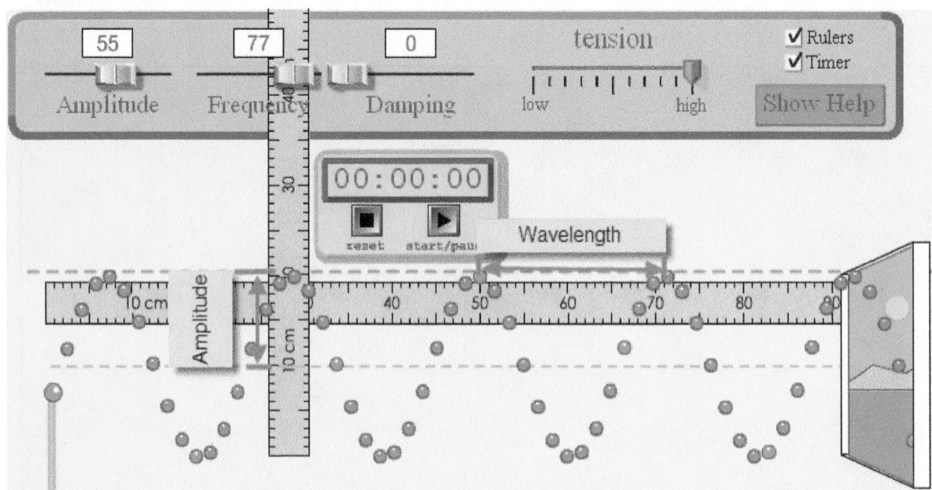

Figure 9-8

6. Leave the simulation paused. In the last step, you placed the vertical ruler at the midpoint of a crest of the wave. Leave the ruler in that same position. Make sure your timer—see Figure 9-4—is set to zero, t_1. Use the step button—see Figure 9-6—to step

the time until the next crest is in the middle of the vertical ruler. Note the time, t_2. Calculate the period of the wave.

Time: _________ s

7. Calculate the frequency.

Frequency: __________ Hz

8. Adjust the following settings to the simulation:

a. Set *Amplitude* to **25**.
b. Set *Frequency* to **75**.
c. Leave all other settings the same.
d. Click the *Reset* button.
e. Click *reset* on the *Timer*.
f. Click *pause/play* to stop the wave motion.
g. Realign your Rulers and Reference Line as instructed in Step 4.

9. Sketch the wave below:

10. Measure the wavelength as described in Step 4.

Wavelength: _______ cm

11. Measure the amplitude as described in Step 5.

Amplitude: _______ cm

12. Calculate the period as described in Step 6.

    Time: ________ s

13. Calculate the frequency.

    Frequency: ________ Hz

Part 2: Pulse Waves

1. Apply the following settings to the simulation:

    a. Click the *Reset* button.
    b. Turn **off** the *Measurement Tools.*
    c. Set *Wave Selector* to **Pulse.**
    d. Set *End Type* to **Fixed End.**
    e. Set *Amplitude* to **50.**
    f. Set *Pulse Width* to **50.**
    g. Set *Damping* to **0.**
    h. Set *Tension* to **High.**
    i. Check both boxes on the *Measurement Tools* panel: *Rulers* and *Timer.*

    If you have correctly applied the settings, your screen will look similar to Figure 9-9.

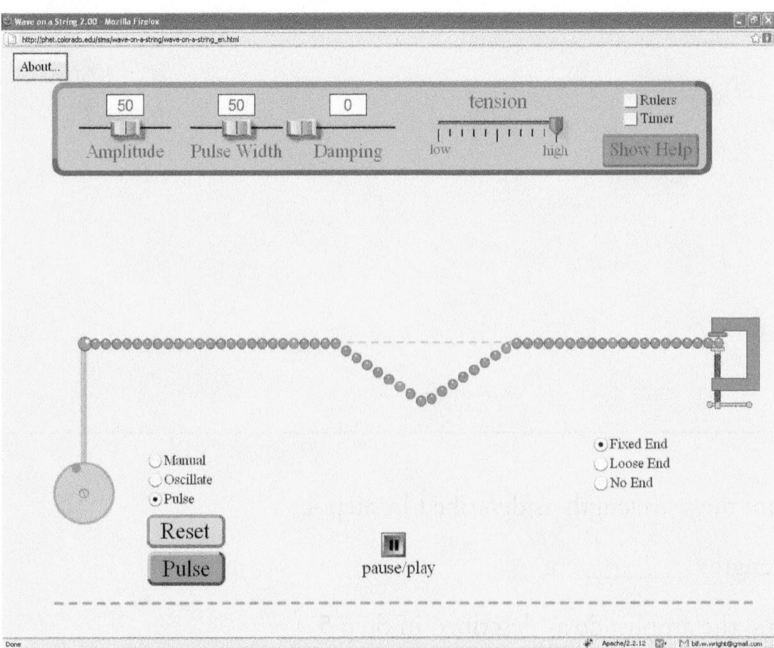

Figure 9-9

2. Click the *Pulse* button. A wave will begin to move through the string, as shown in Figure 9-9.
3. Describe what the wave does as it moves down the string. After it hits the end of the string, what happens to the wave?

4. Click the *Reset* button. Keep the same settings as in Part 2 Step 1 **except** set *End Type* to **Loose End** as shown in Figure 9-10.

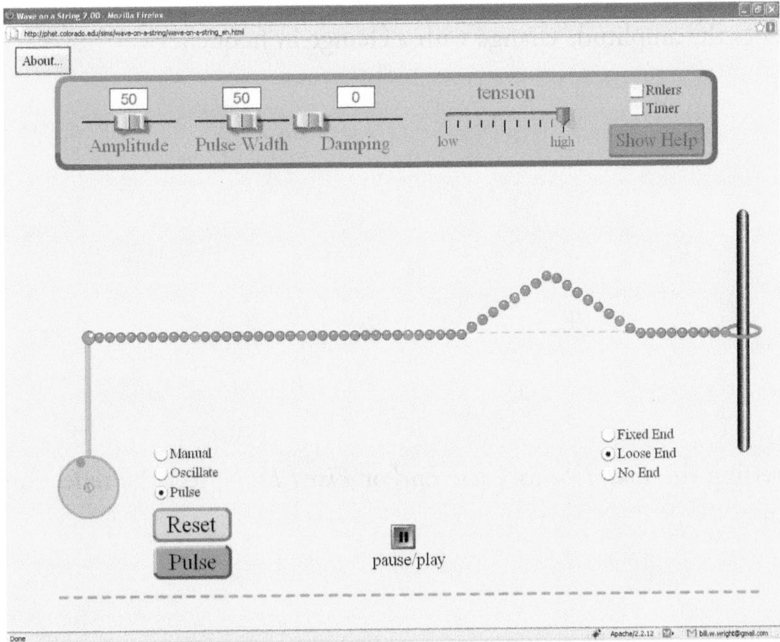

Figure 9-10

5. Click the *Pulse* button.
6. Describe what the wave does as it moves down the string. After it hits the end, what happens to the wave?

QUESTIONS

1. How does the wavelength change as the frequency of the wave changes?

2. How does the amplitude change with a change in frequency?

3. Does setting the *End Type* to *Loose End* or *Fixed End* affect the reflection of the wave? Explain.

10

QUANTUM THEORY

PURPOSE

The purpose of this lab is to investigate the photoelectric effect.

SIMULATIONS

The Photoelectric Effect

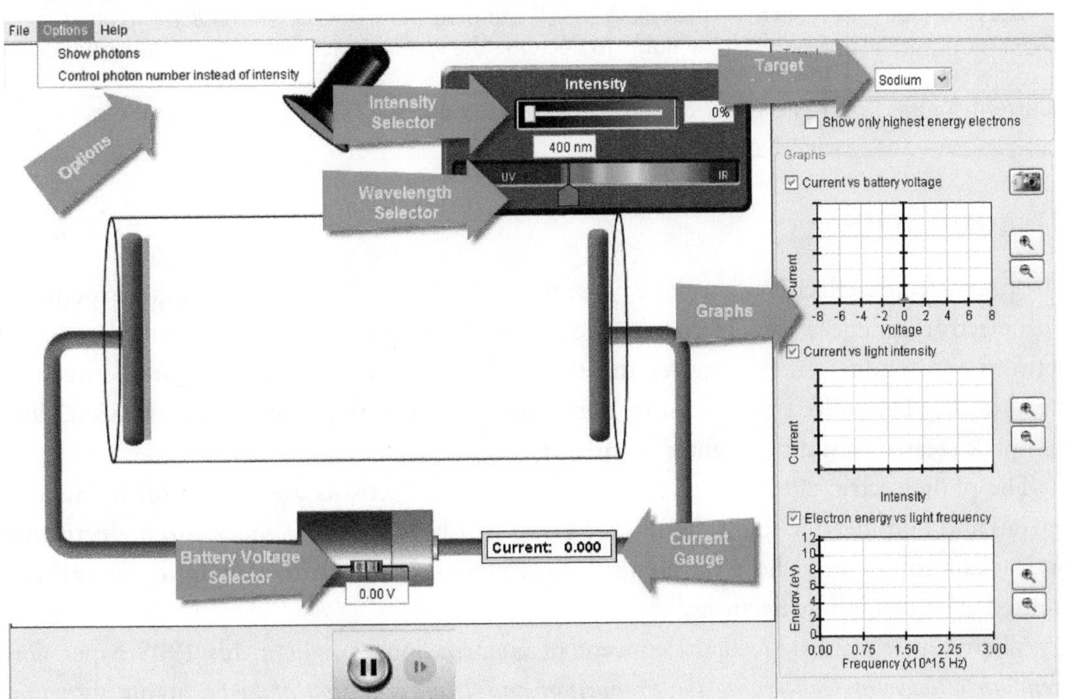

Figure 10-1

Feature	Control
Figure 10-1	
Options	For this lab, you will need to select *Show* photons from the pull down *Options* menu.
Wavelength Selector	Click and drag the slider bar on the *Wavelength Selector* left or right to make a color choice.
Target	Use the Target pull-down menu to select a material for the experiment.
Graphs	When you start the simulation, the graphs on the Graph panel will be hidden, as shown in Figure 10-2. For this lab, enable all of the graphs by checking the boxes beside the name of each graph. Graphs ☐ Current vs battery voltage ☐ Current vs light intensity ☐ Electron energy vs light frequency Figure 10-2
Battery Voltage Selector	To increase the voltage, click and drag the slider bar on the *Battery Voltage Selector* to the right. To decrease the voltage, click and drag the slider bar on the *Battery Voltage Selector* to the left.
Current Gauge	You can see the current passing through the circuit by looking at the current gauge.

INTRODUCTION

The photoelectric effect was accidently discovered by Heinrich Hertz during his experiments with electromagnetic waves. Hertz was producing electromagnetic pluses by creating a spark between two conductors. He detected the wave while measuring an induced spark between two metal knobs. He noticed that when he illuminated the detecting knobs with ultraviolet light, the spark created would be brighter in intensity.

The photoelectric effect is a phenomenon in which **electrons** are thrown off by materials (metals and non-metallic solids, liquids, or gases) that have absorbed energy from **electromagnetic radiation** of very short **wavelength**, such as **visible** or **ultraviolet light**. We call these emitted electrons "photoelectrons."

Albert Einstein introduced the concept of quantization of light in his 1905 paper *On a Heuristic Viewpoint Concerning the Production and Transformation of Light*, about absorption and emission of light. Einstein's explanation of the photoelectric effect won him the **Nobel Prize in Physics** in 1921.

Einstein extended Max Planck's hypothesis about discrete portions (quanta) of energy generated by thermal oscillators and applied this idea to explain the photoelectric effect:

$$E_n = n \cdot (h \cdot f)$$

where $h = 6.6260755 \times 10^{-34} J \cdot s$ is the **Planck constant** ($n = 1,2,3, \ldots$).

Einstein's photoelectric equation describes the kinetic energy of an electron ejected from the body by the incident radiation:

$$K.E. = h \cdot f - W$$

where f is the frequency of the incident photon. In this equation, $W = h \cdot f_0$ is the work function, which is the minimum energy required to remove an electron from a material, and f_0 is called the threshold frequency for the material.

In this lab, you will investigate the effect of light on various materials and measure the flow of electrons in circuits utilizing these materials. The electrons will be created using the photoelectric effect.

PROCEDURES

Part 1: Sodium

1. Apply the following settings to the simulation:

   a. Set the *Intensity Selector* to **0%**.
   b. Set the *Wavelength Selector* to the color purple—**400nm**.
   c. Set the *Battery Voltage Selector* to **3V**.
   d. Check all three graphs on the *Graph* panel so they are all visible.
   e. On the *Target* pull-down menu, select **Sodium**.
   f. Set *Options* to **Show photons**.

   If you have correctly applied the settings, your screen will look similar to Figure 10-3.

2. Slowly increase the intensity to 30%. Describe what happens to the current, voltage, and energy. What are the values of energy and current at 30%?

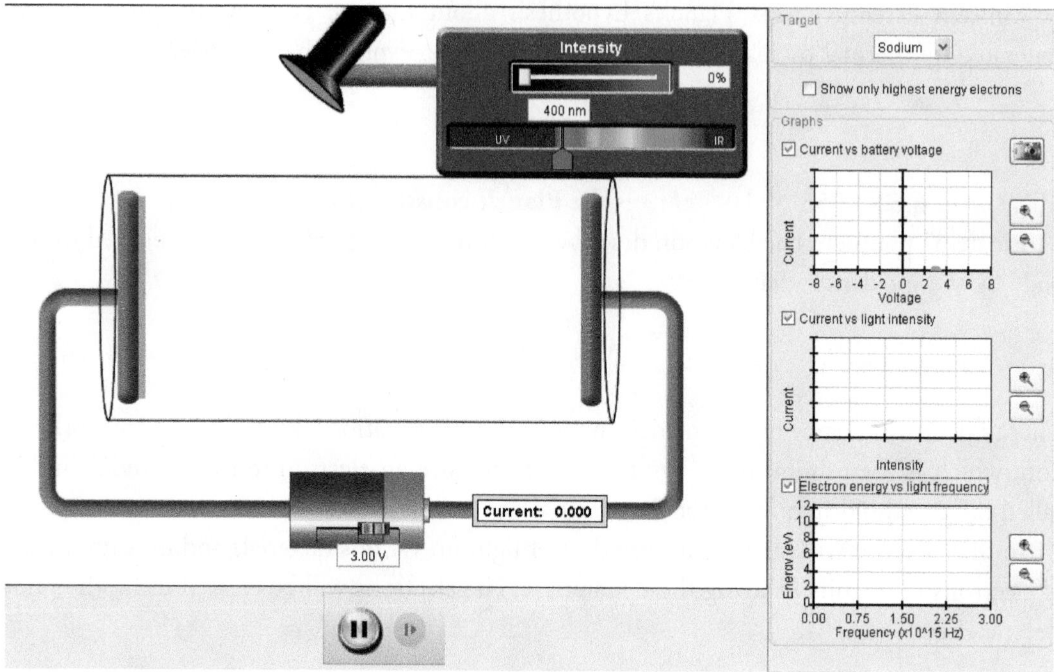

Figure 10-3

3. Now increase the intensity to 100%. What happens to the current, voltage, and energy as you increase the intensity to 100%?

4. Explain why the electrons leave the plate on the left and move to the right. How do these electrons free themselves from the plate?

5. Change the intensity back to 30%. Change the wavelength to green (approximately 510nm). Describe the effect this has on the current, and energy.

6. Change the *Wavelength Selector* to UV (268nm). Describe the effect this has on the current and energy in relation to the readings from the previous step.

7. Find the kinetic energy of the electrons and compare it to the graph of electron energy vs. light frequency. You will need the following conversion factors, constants, and formulas to calculate the kinetic energy. **Show your work.**

   For sodium, W = 2.17eV.
   $1.00\ eV = 1.60 \times 10^{-19} J$
   $1.00\ nm = 1.00 \times 10^{-9}\ m$
   $h = 6.63 \times 10^{-34} J \cdot s$ (Planck's constant)

   $c = 3.00 \times 10^{8} \frac{m}{s}$ (speed of light in a vacuum)

   $f = \frac{c}{\lambda}$ (λ is a wavelength, f is a frequency of light in a vacuum)

   $K.E. = h \cdot f - W$ ($K.E.$ is kinetic enegry of a photoelectron,
   W is the work function)

$f =$ ________________ Hz

$W =$ ________________ J

$K.E. =$ ________________ eV

Part 2: Copper and Platinum

8. Keep the intensity at 30%. Change the *Target* pull-down menu to **Copper**. Find the wavelength of light that gives the highest current. What are the values for the wavelength, current, and energy?

   Wavelength = ____________ nm

   Current = ______________ A

   Energy = ______________ J

9. Keep the intensity at 30%. Change the *Target* pull-down menu to **Platinum**. Find the wavelength of light that gives the highest current. What are the values for the wavelength, current, and energy?

   Wavelength = ____________ nm

   Current = ______________ A

   Energy = ______________ J

QUESTIONS

1. How do the wavelength of the light, the energy of the light, and the current compare between platinum and copper in Steps 8 and 9?

2. How does the battery voltage affect the experiment?

3. Can current flow exist without a voltage on the battery?

11

ELECTROMAGNETIC LAB

PURPOSE

The purpose of this lab is to explore the strength of the magnetism field near a bar magnet, and the magnetic field generated by electric currents. The lab also provides the opportunity to explore the concept of electromagnetic induction (Faraday's Law).

SIMULATIONS

Faraday's Electromagnetic Lab

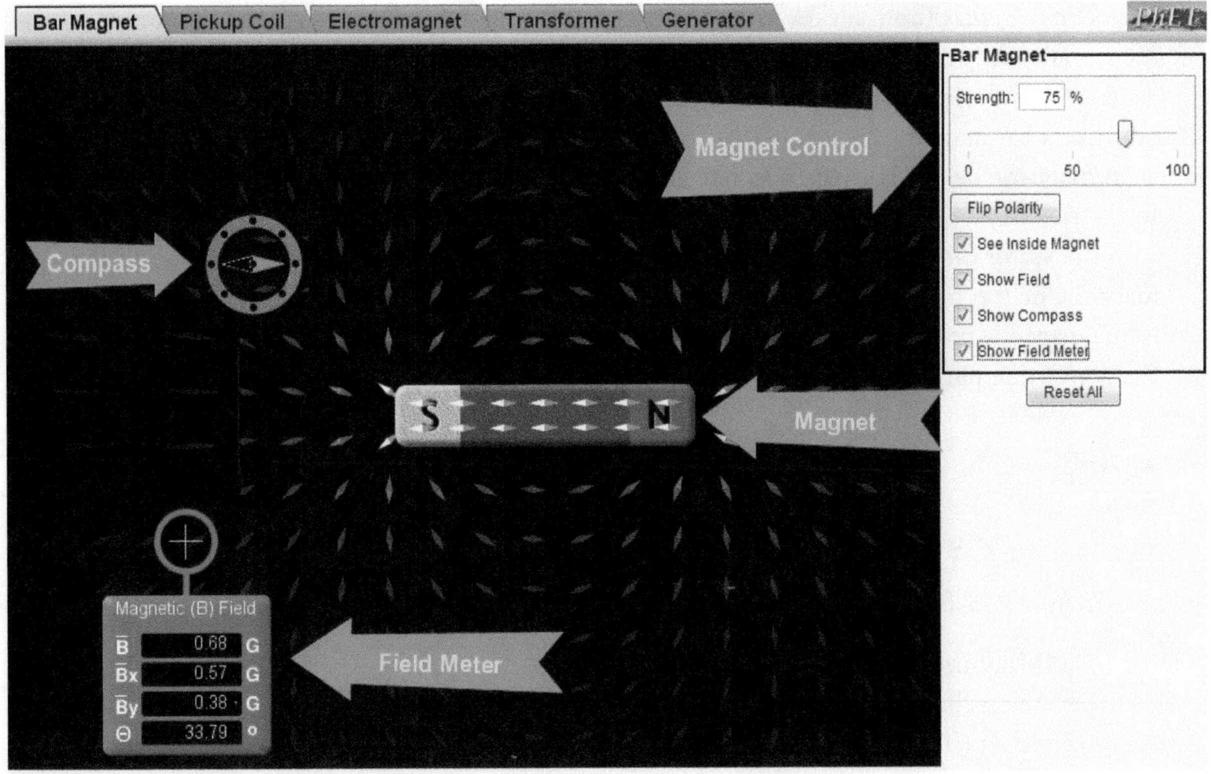

Figure 11-1: Bar Magnet Tab

Feature	Control
Figure 11-1: Bar Magnet Tab	
Options	For this lab, you will need to select all the options on the *Magnet Control* as shown in Figure 11-1.
Strength	Use the *Strength* slider bar on the *Magnet Control* to adjust the strength of the magnet.
Field Meter	When you start the simulation, the Field Meter will be hidden. You must select *Show Field Meter* on the *Magnet Control* to see this feature appear on the screen. Click and drag the object to move it.
Magnet	Click and drag the Magnet to move it.
Compass	Click and drag the Compass to move it.

INTRODUCTION

This lab provides an opportunity to explore magnetism and how magnetism is produced by electric currents. A moving charge is found to create a magnetic field in its vicinity. Atoms have many moving electrons, each electron creating its own magnetic field. In most cases, however, this motion is averaged out and there is little or no effect. Some atoms, however, do not cancel the field due to the coordinated spinning of the outer orbital electrons. These are the ferromagnetic materials (iron, nickel, and cobalt) and they exhibit permanent magnetic properties such as attracting nails or other magnets (such as a small compass). Magnetic fields can also be generated by electric currents in regular wires. A loop carrying DC current behaves fundamentally like a bar magnet.

A magnetic field $\overline{\boldsymbol{B}}$ is a vector, so like all vectors, it has an x and a y component, B_x *and* B_y. In the vicinity of a bar magnet, the magnitude of the magnetic field and the angle θ associated with the vector can be measured. The unit of magnetic field is the Tesla (T). Another unit for magnetic field is the Gauss (G), which is used in this lab. To have an idea how strong a Gauss is, the magnetic field on the surface of the Earth (a big magnet on its own) is about half a Gauss. For converting purposes, $1\ T = 10^4\ G$.

PROCEDURES

Part 1: Bar Magnet

1. Apply the following settings to the simulation:

    a. Maximize the screen.
    b. Select the *Bar Magnet* tab.
    c. Select (check) all options on the *Magnet Control* panel.

    If you have correctly applied the settings, your screen will look similar to Figure 11-1.

2. Use the slider bar on the *Magnet Control* panel to adjust the magnet strength to read between 80 and 100%. Place the CROSS of the *Field Meter* at location roughly 1″ TO THE RIGHT AND ½″ ABOVE the north pole of the magnet. See Figure 11-2.

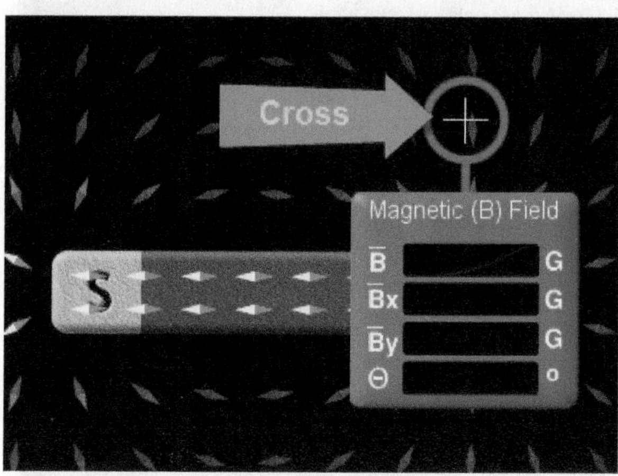

Figure 11-2

3. Write the values that appear in the *Field Meter* in the blanks below:

a. $\overline{\mathbf{B}}$ 3.21 G
b. $\overline{\mathbf{B}}x$ 0.01 G
c. $\overline{\mathbf{B}}y$ 3.21 G
d. (angle) θ 89.88°

4. Substitute these values into this equation to show that $\overline{\mathbf{B}}x^2 + \overline{\mathbf{B}}y^2 = \overline{\mathbf{B}}^2$.

$(0.01)^2 + (3.21)^2 = 10.3042$

0.01 10.3041

$\theta = \tan^{-1}\left(\frac{3.21}{0.01}\right)$

$= 0.809784$

5. Show that the angle $\theta = \tan^{-1}(\overline{\mathbf{B}}y/\overline{\mathbf{B}}x)$.

6. Now move the magnet to the far left of the screen and place the cross of the field meter touching the edge of the N pole of the magnets. See Figure 11-3.

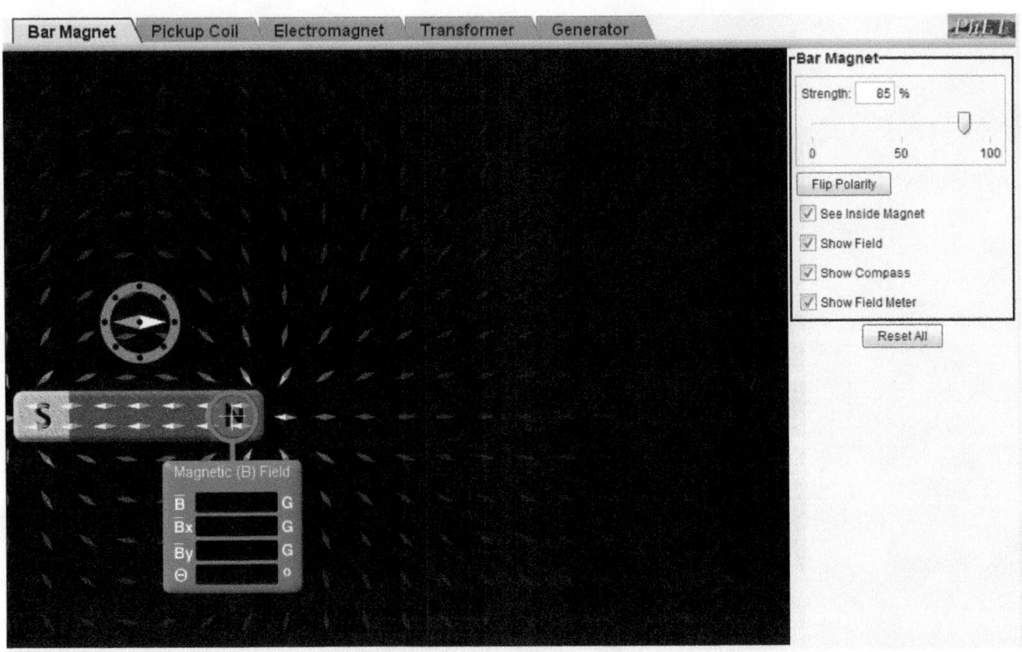

Figure 11-3

Notice that the field markers (the little compasses filling the screen) are located at an equal distance from each other. Let's call that distance *d*. Place the cross of the *Field Meter* on each field marker along a straight line to the right of the N pole, up to a distance of 10*d* (10 field markers). Record the values of $\overline{\mathbf{B}}$ in the table below:

Distance (in units of d)	0	1	2	3	4	5	6	7	8	9	10
$\overline{\mathbf{B}}$ (G)	207.30	70.90	11.79	4.04	1.87	1.02	0.64	6.44	0.31	0.23	0.17

7. Plot the data using the grid at the end of this lab exercise labeled Part 1 Step 7. Place the $\overline{\mathbf{B}}$ field values along the vertical axis and the distance along the horizontal axis. Plot the points, then join them into a smooth line or curve.

Part 2: Electromagnet

1. Apply the following settings to the simulation:

    a. Maximize the screen.
    b. Select the *Electromagnet* tab.
    c. In the control panel on the right, choose *Current Source* = DC.
    d. Choose *Loops* = 1.
    e. Select (check) all options on the electromagnet control panel.

    If you have correctly applied the settings, your screen will look similar to Figure 11-4.

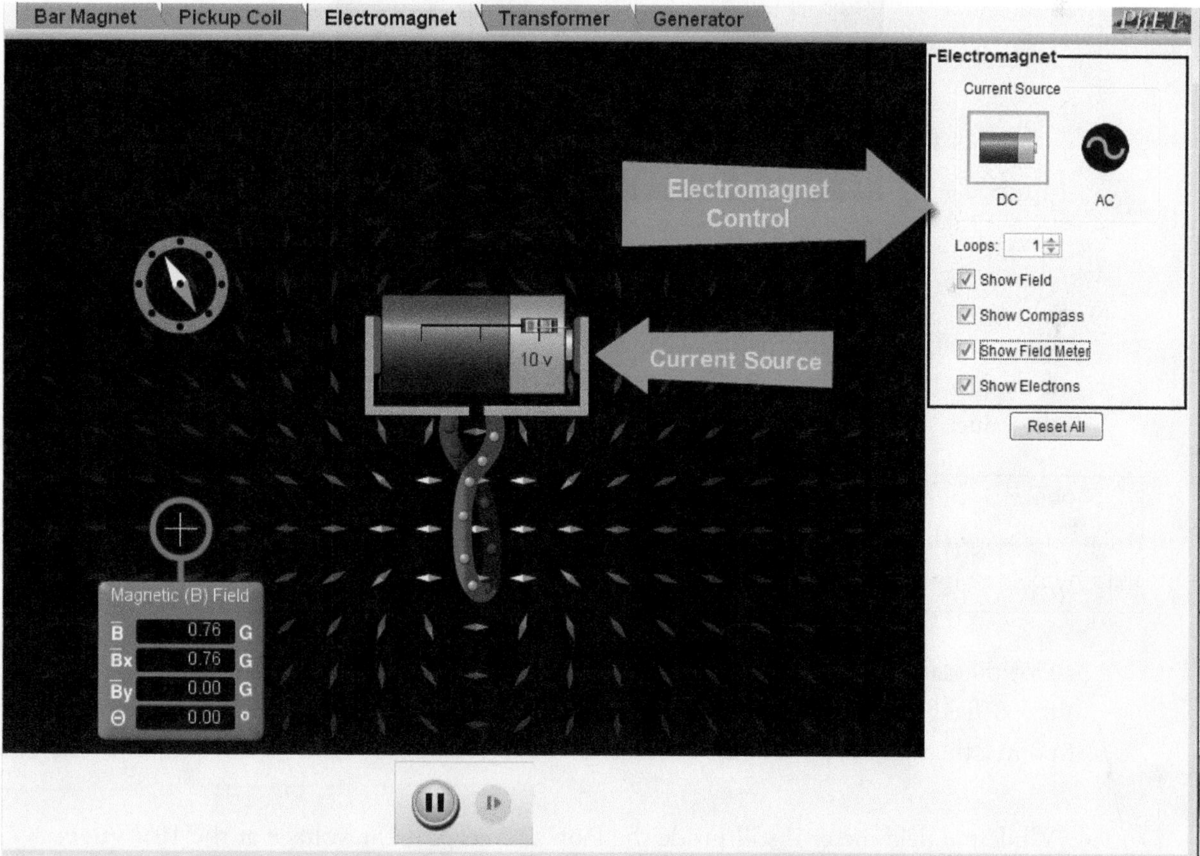

Figure 11-4: Electromagnetic Tab

2. Place the cross of the field meter inside the loop below the battery (*Current Source*). See Figure 11-5.

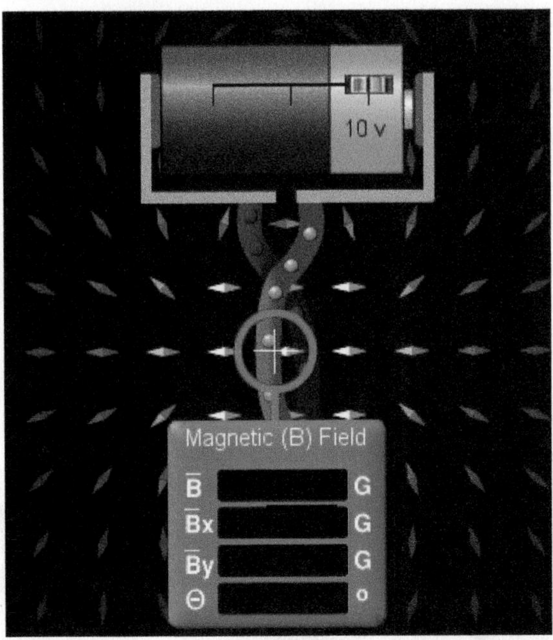

Figure 11-5

Using the *Current Source Switch*, change the value of the DC source (positive values only from 0 to 10V). Record the values of $\overline{\mathbf{B}}x$ (in Gauss) in the following table as you change the value:

Voltage 1 loop	0	1	2	3	4	5	6	7	8	9	10
$\overline{\mathbf{B}}x$ (G)	0	7.50	15.00	22.50	30.00	37.50	45.00	52.50	60.00	67.50	75.50

3. Plot the data using the grid at the end of this lab exercise labeled Part 2 Step 3. Place the $\overline{\mathbf{B}}$ field values along the vertical axis and volts along the horizontal axis. Plot the points, then join them into a smooth line or curve.

4. While the field meter is still inside the loop and keeping the voltage at the 10V value, change the number of loops from Step 1 from 1 to 4. Record the values of $\overline{\mathbf{B}}$ in the table below.

# Loops at 10V	1	2	3	4
$\overline{\mathbf{B}}x$ (G)	75.00	150.00	225.00	300.00

In the space below, speculate on the relationship between the strength of the field and the number of loops. the more loops the stronger the field and more positive charge from it.

5. Now change the *Current Source* to AC. Use the frequency adjusting slider bars to make the frequency of the graph as low as possible (but greater than zero). What happens to the value of $\overline{\mathbf{B}}$x inside the loop? (Notice that the values of $\overline{\mathbf{B}}$ and $\overline{\mathbf{B}}$x are identical in this case, while $\overline{\mathbf{B}}$y equals zero.) it goes back and forth from positive to negative.

Part 3: Transformer

1. Select the *Transformer* tab. Your screen should look like Figure 11-6.

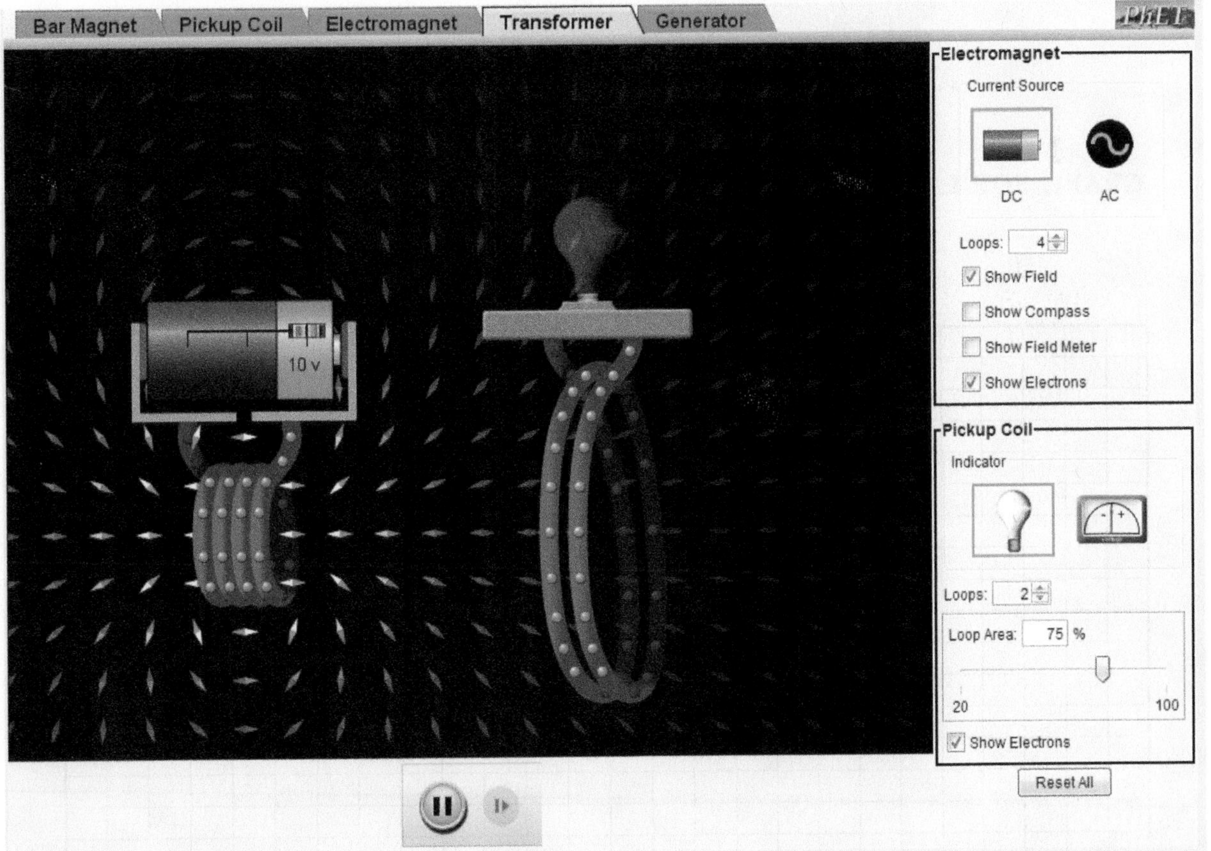

Figure 11-6: Transformer Tab

2. In this part of the lab, you are free to investigate the way scientists do: without instructions. Explore all the variables in this experiment and see how they affect the brightness of the light bulb. Record all your observations as a series of precise, brief statements. Remember to change one variable at a time while keeping the others constant. In each case, report what happens to the brightness of the bulb.

   Use the space below to record your observations.

GRAPH FOR LAB 11

Part 1 Step 7

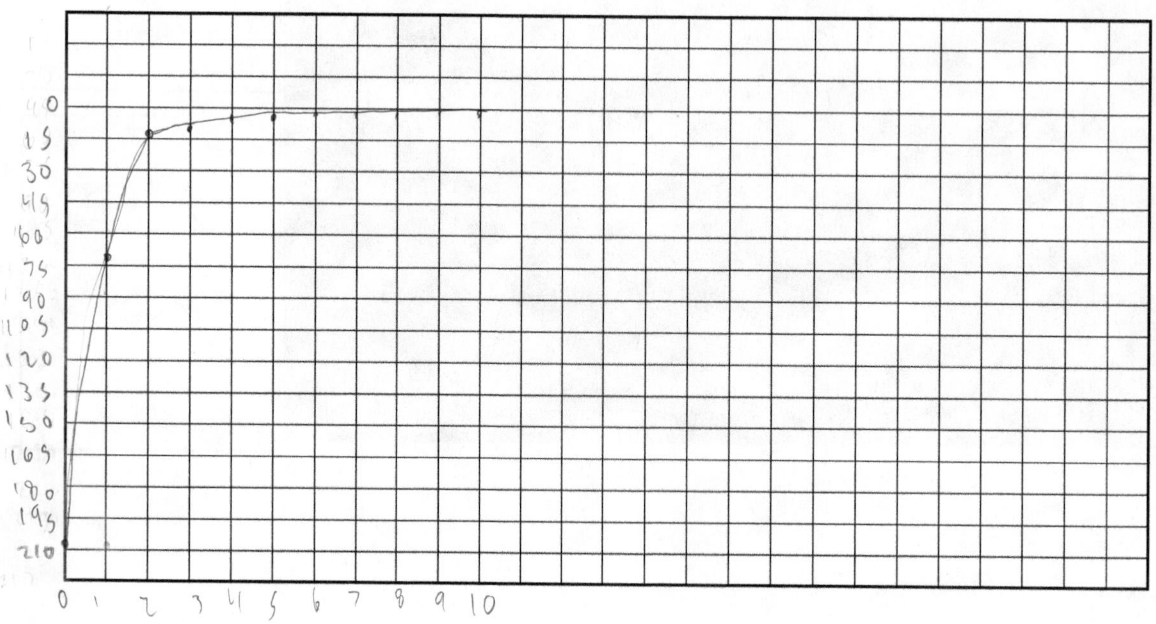

Part 2 Step 3

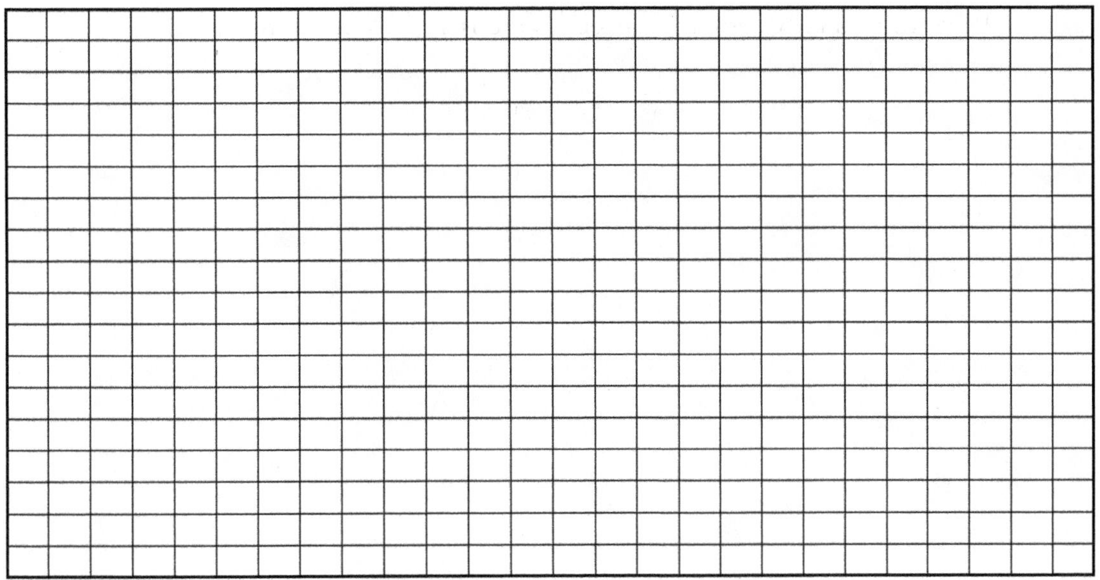

TROUBLESHOOTING

This troubleshooting guide will help you solve some of the problems people commonly have running the PhET simulations. ***These tips were taken from the PhET Web site in October, 2009. For the most up-to-date and dynamic instructions, please visit the site at http://phet.colorado.edu/tech_support/index.php***

FAQs

- Why can I run some of the simulations but not all?
- What are the System Requirements for running PhET simulations?
- I use Internet Explorer and the simulations do not run on my computer.
- Why don't Flash simulations run on my computer?
- What is the ideal screen resolution to run PhET simulations?
- I have Windows 2000 and can run Flash simulations but the Java based simulations do not work.
- Why do PhET simulations run slower on my laptop than on a desktop?
- Why does my computer crash when I run a simulation that has sound?
- What are licensing requirements?

Why Can I Run Some of the Simulations but Not All?

Some of the PhET simulations are Java Web Start-based applications and others use Macromedia's Flash player. Flash comes with most computers while Java Web Start is a free application that you can download from Sun Microsystems. To run the Java-based simulations, you must have Java version 1.5 or higher installed on your computer. To download Java, go to *http://java.sun.com/javase/downloads/index.jsp*, or start at the Sun Microsystems home page (*www.sun.com*) and follow the links for downloads.

What are the System Requirements to Run PhET Simulations?

Windows Systems:

- Intel Pentium processor
- Microsoft Windows 98SE/2000/XP/Vista
- 256MB RAM minimum
- Approximately 98 MB available disk space (for full installation)
- 1024 × 768 screen resolution or better
- Sun Java 1.5.0_15 or later
- Macromedia Flash 8 or later
- Microsoft Internet Explorer 6 or later, Firefox 2 or later

I Use Internet Explorer and the Simulations Do Not Run on My Computer.

It is ***strongly*** recommended that you use Internet Explorer 7 or newer.

Internet Explorer Security Settings

Some installations of Internet Explorer, particularly under Windows XP SP2, have default security settings that can impede some aspects of how your locally installed PhET interface functions. For the best user experience while using PhET simulations installed on your computer, we recommend following the steps below:

1. In Internet Explorer on your local workstation, choose Tools>Internet Options.
2. Choose the Advanced tab, then scroll to the Security section.
3. Enable "Allow active content to run in files on my computer."
4. Choose OK.

Why Don't Flash Simulations Run on My Computer?

QuickTime™ and Flash™ Compatibility

Some users are unable to use our Flash-based simulations because of a compatibility issue between Apple Computer's QuickTime and the Flash player. Some users have reported that uninstalling QuickTime resolves the issue.

What is the Ideal Screen Resolution to Run PhET Simulations?

PhET simulations work best at a screen resolution of 1024 × 768 pixels. (Some of them are written so that they cannot be resized.) At lower resolution (e.g., 800 × 600), all the controls may not fit on your screen. At higher resolution (e.g., 1280 × 1024), you may not be able to make the simulation fill the whole screen, or if you do, it may slow down performance. To change your screen resolution, follow the directions below:

Windows Vista

1. From the Start menu, click on Control Panel.
2. Under Appearance and Personalization, click "Adjust screen resolution."
3. Use the Screen resolution slider to select a resolution and click OK.

Windows 98SE/2000/XP

1. From Start menu, click on Control Panel.
2. Double-click on the Display icon.
3. Select the Settings tab.
4. Use the Screen resolution slider to select a resolution and click OK.

I have Windows 2000 and can Run Flash Simulations but the Java-Based Simulations Do Not Work.

Some Windows 2000 systems have been reported to lack part of the necessary Java configuration. These systems will typically start our Flash-based simulations reliably, but will appear to do nothing when launching our Java-based simulations.

To Resolve this Situation, Please Perform the Following Steps:

1. From the desktop or start menu, open My Computer.
2. In the Tools menu, click on the Folder Options item.
3. At the top of the window that appears, click on the File Types tab.
4. In the extensions column, locate JNLP and click it once to select the item.
5. Click on the Change button.
6. When asked to choose which program to use to open JNLP files, select Browse.
7. Locate the program javaws or javaws.exe in your Java installation folder (typically C:\Program Files\Java\j2re1.xxxx\javaws, where "xxxx" is a series of numbers indicating the software version; choose the latest version).
8. Select the program file and then click Open to use the javaws program to open JNLP files.

Java-based simulations should now function properly.

Why Do PhET Simulations Run Slower on My Laptop than on a Desktop?

On some laptop computers, simulations may appear to run much slower than anticipated and/or exhibit unexpected graphics problems. This may be due to power management settings that affect how the computer's graphics system runs. You can correct this situation by either a) changing the computer's power management configuration, or b) using the laptop computer while plugged in to an AC power source.

Many laptop computers are configured to reduce the amount of power used by the graphics/video system while the computer is running on battery power. If you must use the laptop while it is not plugged in, we suggest changing your computer's power management settings to "maximize performance" while it is unplugged. This should ensure that the graphics system runs at its peak speed. The location of this setting varies from one manufacturer to the next; if you have difficulty locating it, we suggest contacting your computer vendor.

Why Does My Computer Crash When I Run a Simulation That Has Sound?

Simulations that use sound can be unstable when run on computers using old device driver software. If you are encountering crashes or other undesirable behavior with any of our simulations that use sound, we advise updating your sound drivers, as this may solve the problem.

TROUBLESHOOTING JAVA

PhET's Java-based simulations use Sun Microsystems' Java Web Start technology to launch the simulations. This page will help you ensure that you have Java installed properly, and address some of the problems people might have running our programs.

FAQs

- How do I get Java?
- Why do you use Java Web Start instead of Java?
- How do I check my computer's current version of Java?
- I have Windows 2000 and I can only get the Flash-based simulations to work.
- General Java troubleshooting
- Troubleshooting tips for networked computers

How Do I Get Java?

To run the Java-based simulations, you must have Java version 1.5 or higher installed on your computer. You can obtain the free downloads by clicking on the button below located on the PhET Web site.

Note for Netscape Users
After you have installed Java Web Start, you will need to close and re-open your browser for Java Web Start to work.

Why Do You Use Java Web Start Instead of Java?

We use Java Web Start technology rather than Java Applets. Java Web Start, which is a free mechanism from Sun, is a more robust way of launching Java programs over the Web than applets. If you have had problems running applets in the past, you may well find that Java Web Start works much better. If you should have any problems, we will be happy to help you solve them.

How Do I Check My Computer's Current Version of Java?

Windows Vista Users

From a command line (Start menu>All Programs>Accessories>Command Prompt), type: **javaws -viewer** then press Enter. You should see some text that will include something like "(build 1.4.2_05_05-b04)"; this number is the version of Java you are using. If you receive an error, Java is not properly installed. (See above for reinstallation instructions.)

Windows 98SE/2000/XP Users

From a command line (Start menu>All Programs>Accessories>Command Prompt), type: **java -version** and press Enter. You should see some text that will include something like "(build 1.4.2_05_05-b04)"; this number is the version of Java you are using. If you receive an error, Java is not properly installed. (See above for reinstallation instructions.)

I Have Windows 2000 and I Can Only Get the Flash-Based Simulations to Work.

Some Windows 2000 systems have been reported to lack part of the necessary Java configuration. These systems will typically start our Flash-based simulations reliably, but will appear to do nothing when launching our Java-based simulations.

To Resolve this Situation, Please Perform the Following Steps:

1. From the desktop or start menu, open My Computer.
2. In the Tools menu, click on Folder Options.
3. At the top of the window that appears, click on the File Types tab.
4. Locate JNLP in the extensions column, and click it once to select the item.
5. Click on the Change button.
6. When asked to choose which program to use to open JNLP files, select Browse.
7. Locate the program javaws or javaws.exe in your Java installation folder (typically C:\Program Files\Java\j2re1.xxxx\javaws, where "xxxx" is a series of numbers indicating the software version; choose the latest version).
8. Select the program file and then click Open to use the javaws program to open JNLP files.

General Java Troubleshooting

The following are some general steps that you may wish to perform when attempting to solve Java-related problems:

- **Empty Your Browser's Cache.**

  Internet Explorer

  From the toolbar, select Tools>Options, then click on the Delete Files... button under Temporary Internet Files.

  Firefox

  Select Tools>Options>Privacy, then click the Clear button next to Cache.

- **Empty Java Web Start's Cache.**
  From Windows Start menu, select Java Web Start, then select Preferences from the File menu. Click Advanced, then click the Clear Folder button.

- **Make Sure Windows can find Java and Java Web Start.**
  From a command line (Start menu>Accessories>Command Prompt), type *java -version* followed by the enter key. If you receive an error, Java is not properly installed. Please try reinstalling Java (see above) after uninstalling any Java entries in your list of installed programs (Control Panel>Add/Remove Programs).

Troubleshooting Tips for Networked Computers

Why Do Simulations Run for Admin but Not All Users?
Java simulations may also fail to start on networked computers running Windows for some users while running properly for administrators. When Java Web Start tries to launch a simulation, it attempts to cache certain files in a cache folder. This folder (or directory) is determined when Java is installed, and may point to a folder that non-administrator accounts do not have access to, resulting in a launch failure. Correct this problem by setting the cache directory to one of your own choosing: Log on as an administrator.

Launch the Java Web Start Application Manager. This can be done in one of two ways:

a) If the Java installation placed an icon either on your desktop or in the Start Menu>All Programs list titled Java Web Start, click it to start the application.

b) Use the Windows search function (located in the Start Menu) to search for the program javaws.exe. Once it is found, click on the file to run the application. Once the Java Web Start Application Manager is up and running, choose File>Preferences. In the Preferences dialog that appears, click on the Advanced tab. In this tab, you will find a text field labeled Applications Folder. In this text field, put the name of an empty directory to which all users have write privileges. Note: This directory MUST be empty. All users should now be able to launch the Java simulations.

Issue 3: Web Proxy Settings

Java simulations may fail to start if the proxy settings in Java Web Start's configuration panel (Start Menu>Java Web Start, File Menu>Preferences) do not match those your system is currently using. To identify settings being used on your system, see your web browser's proxy settings, or contact you network administrator.

Local Install on Boot Drive Only

If you are operating in a networked environment, please ensure that both Java and the PhET simulations (if installed locally rather than running from our web site) are installed on local, non-networked drives. The PhET simulations must be installed on the boot drive.

Network Firewalls

Please ensure that your firewall is configured to allow both Java and Java Web Start to communicate through the firewall.

TROUBLESHOOTING FLASH

To run the Flash-based simulations, you must have Macromedia Flash 8 (available free) or newer installed on your computer.

If you get a blank window when you try to launch a Flash simulation, you probably need a new version of the Flash player.

Older versions of the Flash Player can cause problems. Updating your Flash player is recommended if you receive an error similar to:

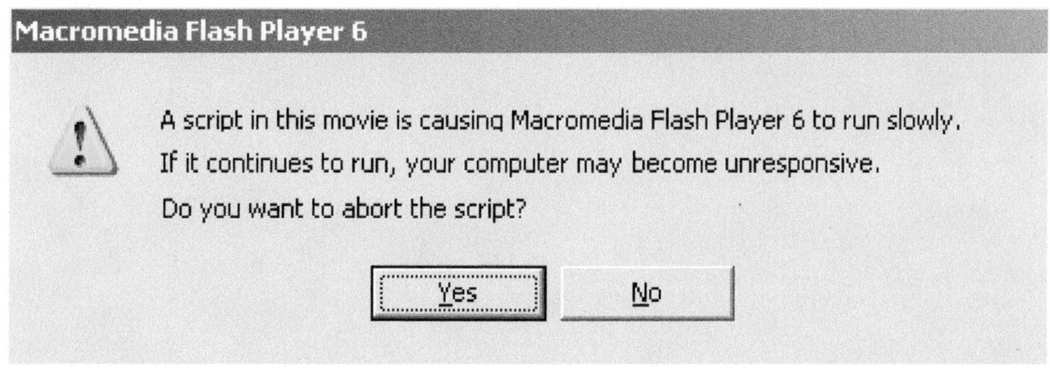

TROUBLESHOOTING JAVASCRIPT

JavaScript is a programming language primarily used in Web pages, usually to add features that make the page more interactive. JavaScript is required to submit information to PhET. All JavaScript troubleshooting is dynamic. Instructions are available in the troubleshooting section of the PhET Web site (http://phet.colorado.edu/tech_support/index.php).